CE National, Inc.
1003 Presidential Dr.
P. O. Box 365
Winona Lake, IN 46590

This is Bob Lepine at his best, teaching men how to bring the best out of the woman God has called them to love, lead and honor.

DR. TIM KIMMEL

AUTHOR, *BASIC TRAINING FOR A FEW GOOD MEN*

A challenge to men to be the husbands God has called us to be: sacrificial, servant leaders. This book delivers both the tools and the encouragement to fulfill the biblical calling on every Christian husband.

DR. GARY ROSBERG

AUTHOR, *GUARD YOUR HEART*

Bob Lepine is a thinker and has a great sense of humor, qualities that make this a refreshing book.

STU WEBER

AUTHOR, *TENDER WARRIOR: GOD'S INTENTION FOR A MAN*

BOB LEPINE

The CHRISTIAN HUSBAND

Regal

From Gospel Light
Ventura, California, U.S.A.

CE National, Inc.
1003 Presidential Dr
P. O. Box 365
Winona Lake, IN 46590

PUBLISHED BY REGAL BOOKS
FROM GOSPEL LIGHT
VENTURA, CALIFORNIA, U.S.A.
PRINTED IN THE U.S.A.

Regal

Regal Books is a ministry of Gospel Light, a Christian publisher dedicated to serving the local church. We believe God's vision for Gospel Light is to provide church leaders with biblical, user-friendly materials that will help them evangelize, disciple and minister to children, youth and families.

It is our prayer that this Regal book will help you discover biblical truth for your own life and help you meet the needs of others. May God richly bless you.

For a free catalog of resources from Regal Books/Gospel Light, please call your Christian supplier or contact us at 1-800-4-GOSPEL *or* www.regalbooks.com.

All Scripture quotations, unless otherwise indicated, are taken from the *New American Standard Bible,* © 1960, 1962, 1963, 1968, 1971, 1972, 1973, 1975, 1977 by The Lockman Foundation. Used by permission.

Other versions used are
Amer. Std.—American Standard Version, 1901.
NIV—Scripture taken from the *Holy Bible, New International Version®.* Copyright © 1973, 1978, 1984 by International Bible Society. Used by permission of Zondervan Publishing House. All rights reserved.

Servant Publications edition published in 1999.
Regal Books edition published in January 2005.

© 1999 Bob Lepine
All rights reserved.

Cover design by David Griffing
Edited by Amy Spence

Library of Congress Cataloging-in-Publication Data
Lepine, Bob.
  The Christian husband / Bob Lepine.—Regal ed.
     p. cm.
  Includes bibliographical references.
  ISBN 0-8307-3689-1
  1. Husbands—Religious life. 2. Marriage—Religious aspects—Christianity. I. Title.

  BV4528.2.L46 2005
  248.8'425—dc22   2004023943

1   2   3   4   5   6   7   8   9   10   /   10   09   08   07   06   05   04

Rights for publishing this book in other languages are contracted by Gospel Light Worldwide, the international nonprofit ministry of Gospel Light. Gospel Light Worldwide also provides publishing and technical assistance to international publishers dedicated to producing Sunday School and Vacation Bible School curricula and books in the languages of the world. For additional information, visit www.gospellightworldwide.org; write to Gospel Light Worldwide, P.O. Box 3875, Ventura, CA 93006; or send an e-mail to info@gospellightworldwide.org.

DEDICATION

*To the men who may someday come calling, asking to marry
Amy and Kate Lepine. You would do well to read this before you call.
To Jimmy, John and David Lepine. May you, as husbands,
succeed where I have failed.
To Mary Ann. You have affirmed, accepted, encouraged and loved me well.
You know best that I am still learning how to implement what I've written in this
book. Maybe after I read it a few more times, I'll begin to get it right.*

CONTENTS

Part One
The Qualifications of a Christian Husband

Part Two
The Model for Husbands—Jesus Christ

Part Three
The Task—How to Really Love Your Wife

FOREWORD

In the fall of 1992, an experienced broadcaster made a huge decision of faith—a heroic decision to move his family from San Antonio to Little Rock to become the cohost of a daily radio program for families.

This radio program had no name, no stations lined up to air its broadcasts, and its host—me—had virtually no experience on radio. Talk about faith! Let me introduce you to that courageous man, the author of *The Christian Husband*, Bob Lepine.

Because of Bob's leadership, *FamilyLife Today* was born. Now many years later, our radio program is heard in more than 500 communities by more than 1.5 million folks every week.

You really get to know someone when you go through something so challenging and demanding as birthing a "radio baby." Like any growing infant, this daily program required feeding, rocking and, yes, countless diaper changes! Bob stood by the cradle through it all, and I've learned much about him as a man as we've sat together behind the microphone for thousands of broadcasts.

Over the years, I've laughed with him as he's done his Elvis shtick. I've sat around a bonfire, singing songs from the '60s. I'll bet you can't name one that he doesn't know the words to.

Bob and I also have been through a couple of deep and dark valleys together; how a man perseveres under fire tells you a lot about him, and I can tell you that Bob is a good man—a very good man. I learned much by watching Bob keep his wife Mary Ann a priority as he managed his growing brood of five children.

In these pages, Bob peels back his heart and honestly shares the insecurities that every man feels as he takes on the mantle of loving and leading his wife. You'll be able to relate as Bob shares some of his failures and the lessons learned.

Make no mistake—this book is not a fluffy, Bible-lite approach; you're about to receive the biblical job description for becoming a husband. God speaks often and powerfully through His Word in this book, and at the end you won't be left scratching your head about just what God requires of a man who seeks to love and lead his wife.

If you've ever wondered as a man what it means, practically, to love your wife, then you've found some answers in this book.

If you've been puzzled by how you can practically be the spiritual leader of your wife, look no further. The box top to solve that puzzle is in your hands.

It's time. Strap yourself into your favorite chair and get ready to have your concept of what it means to be a husband challenged and stretched. Like me, you're going to grow to like Bob Lepine and appreciate his ministry in your life.

Yours for a Family Reformation—One Home at a Time,
Dennis Rainey

If I wanted to find out whether a man was a Christian, I wouldn't ask his minister. I would go and ask his wife. If a man doesn't treat his wife right, I don't want to hear him talk about Christianity. What is the use of his talking about salvation for the next life if he has no salvation for this?

D. L. MOODY

ACKNOWLEDGMENTS

In July of 1992, I sat across from Dennis Rainey at a conference room table. We were meeting to discuss the possibility of my coming to FamilyLife to help launch a new daily radio program. After more than 15 years of ministry to families, Dennis was looking for someone who shared his passion for marriage and family.

"Does 'family' make you weep?" he asked. "Does it make you pound the table?"

Did I have a passion for families?

I knew what the answer to that question was supposed to be if I wanted the job! I had a passion for *my* family. But did I have the kind of passion that would be necessary to sustain a daily radio program where we talked about marriage and family issues every day?

The flicker of passion I had on the subject at that meeting has been fanned into a flame in the years since I joined FamilyLife. I have come to see how integral the institution of the family is to everything God has ordained. Before there was a church, before there was a government, before anything else, there was a family. I have come to see that healthy marriages and families are at the top of God's priority list.

My own passion on the subject has been fueled in large measure by Dennis's unwavering passion. In recording more than 1,500 radio programs, I have been mentored, challenged, coached and shaped by his steadfast convictions and his commitment to God's Word. I'm sure that as he read the manuscript for this book, he found himself nodding, as many of his own thoughts are here expressed in my words. It has been a privilege to be both his coworker and his friend over the years.

Special thanks are also due to the team at FamilyLife that holds our radio program together. These are the people who have picked up the slack for me while I've worked on this book: Eric Platner, Keith Lynch, Phil Krause, Mark Ramsey and Andy Watson shape each of our daily broadcasts, with able help from Sheryl Colcough. Mike Clowers returned phone calls to radio stations on my behalf. Tonda Nations assisted in research for this book in the same way she helps prepare us for each radio program. And, as always, Christy Bain keeps the details of my life and my work in order. You guys are a great team. I appreciate you. Now, get back to work.

Thanks, too, to Dave Boehi and Mark Whitlock. Dave is an editor *par excellence*, and his feedback on this manuscript has made it a better book. Mark's advice is always well reasoned and wise beyond its years.

Thanks to the team at Servant for embodying their company name. Special thanks to Bert Ghezzi, who believed in this project from the beginning and who has affirmed me each step of the way.

On Father's Day, 1996, I attended the worship service at Fellowship Bible Church in Tulsa, Oklahoma, where Bruce Ewing is the pastor. It had been years since I'd visited the church we had helped to start. Almost two decades later, I found many friends still there to greet.

The church family had been studying Hebrews and was ready to tackle chapter 8. However, as pastors know, Father's Day is one of the days each year when regular studies are set aside and a special message is preached for the men. That morning, Bruce continued his series in Hebrews, explaining how Christ is both priest and King, and tying that truth to our responsibilities as fathers to be priests and kings in our homes. Much of the middle section of this book germinated from the seeds planted that day.

Throughout the writing of this book, I arrived home many evenings feeling like a hypocrite. As the apostle Paul expressed in Romans 7, I find myself wondering why the things I want to do as a husband continue to go undone. If this book were to be based on my track record as a husband, the advice would last only a few pages. I have tried to center my thoughts on what God's Word has to say about the task, rather than on any sage counsel of my own. My hope is that a reader will learn from what His sure Word has to say to us and will look past my own stuttering tongue on the subject.

Soli deo gloria!

INTRODUCTION

It's a good thing there was no interview. I would never have been given the
job . . .

> "Mr. Lepine, sit down. I have a copy of your résumé right here."
>
> "Thank you, sir."
>
> "You are applying for the position of Mary Ann Alaback's husband,
> is that correct?"
>
> "Yes, sir."
>
> "How old are you, Mr. Lepine?"
>
> "Twenty-three."
>
> "All right. Tell me what you know about the position."
>
> "Well . . . uh . . . I know it's full time, right?"
>
> "That's right."
>
> "And there's a lifetime agreement involved . . . "
>
> "Go on."

"Well, Mary Ann and I will live together, and we'll get to have sex whenever we want, and we'll probably have some children along the way . . . stuff like that."

"Tell me more about what your role in the relationship will be."

"Breadwinner . . . I guess. I mean, she may want to work, or we may wind up needing her to work some, but I guess most of the responsibility for all that will rest with me."

"Anything else?"

"I dunno. There's all the little stuff, like being the one to take out the trash or making sure the oil in the car has been changed. Stuff like that."

"Okay, Mr. Lepine. Let's talk about your qualifications. Have you ever been a husband before?"

"No. In this case, that's good, isn't it?"

"It's preferable. But it does have its downside, too. What kind of experience have you had that prepares you for this position?"

"Uh . . . when I was growing up, I watched a lot of *Father Knows Best* . . . "

"Have you had any formal training?"

"No."

"Have you read any books on the subject?"

"No."

"Have you worked in any related fields?"

"I had a roommate in college. We got along pretty well. And I was a camp counselor for seven summers."

"My question is, do you have any idea how to be a husband?"

"Well, not exactly. But I've learned what not to do by watching some of his mistakes . . . "

"Okay."

"And like I said, I've watched movies and TV shows with husbands in them."

"Okay."

"And what I don't know I can kind of make up as I go along!"

"Mr. Lepine, has anyone read you your job description?"

"Uh . . . no."

"Let me read this to you. You'll be expected to love your wife, 'just as Christ also loved the church and gave Himself up for her; so that He might sanctify her, having cleansed her by the washing of water with the word, that He might present to Himself the church in all her glory, having no spot or wrinkle or any such thing; but that she would be holy and blameless' (Eph. 5:25-27). You'll be expected to love Mary Ann in the same way that you love your own body, to nourish and cherish her just as Christ also does the Church. For this cause you shall leave your father and mother, and shall cleave to your wife; and the two of you shall become one flesh" (see vv. 28-29,31).

"I know about that part."

"Ah . . . yes. Let me continue. You'll be expected to live with your wife in an understanding way, and to grant her honor as a fellow heir of the grace of life, so that your prayers may not be hindered. You'll need to be harmonious, sympathetic, brotherly, kindhearted and humble in spirit; not returning evil for evil, or insult for insult, but giving a blessing instead."

"Whoa. This is a big job!"

"Yes it is, Mr. Lepine. On top of all that, the job is for better or worse. You'll be expected to stick with it, no matter what—illness, injury, financial problems—until one or the other of you dies."

"What if she changes a whole lot?"

"She will."

"Well, how can anyone know if he can stick with something when that job might be totally different 5 or 10 or 20 years from now?"

"It *will* be totally different. And you'll be expected to adapt."

"Listen, all I know is that I love Mary Ann and I want to marry her and I think we make a pretty good team. I can't imagine living life without her."

"That's fine, Mr. Lepine. We hear things like that a lot. Do you
    think you can do the job as I've outlined here?"

"I don't know. I'll try really hard."

"You will fail many times . . ."

"How does anyone ever . . ."

"Few do, Mr. Lepine. It takes a lot of work."

What Is a Husband?

**I became the husband of Mary Ann Alaback at about 10 o'clock in the
morning on Saturday, May 19, 1979.** I had no idea what I was getting
myself into. With an upbeat, confident smile that masked my own
doubts and fears, I stood with my four closest friends and a minister in
a little room off to the right side of the sanctuary, waiting for our cue to
move into the church. My friends were sharing the excitement of the
"big day," while I silently wondered to myself how anyone at age 23
could possibly know enough to make a lifetime commitment to another person.

The title I was given that day—"husband"—is perhaps the most common title given among humankind (tied only with the title of "wife"). It
may be that the very common nature of the title explains why so many
people today are hard pressed to give any kind of a working definition
for what a husband is or what he does.

Most men know that a husband is called in Scripture to love his wife
as Christ loved the Church, but they're not really sure what that means.
It has something to do with sacrifice, of course. But as the apostle Paul
continues his instruction to husbands, it gets a little more confusing
and abstract. Cleansing your wife by the washing of water with the
Word? Presenting her spotless and blameless? Sanctifying her? Loving
your wife as you love your own body? We read the passage, our eyes glaze
a bit, and we skip over the "theological stuff," looking for the easier-to-
understand parts.

In doing so, we end up even more confused about a role we have
signed on to for life. We give this business of being a husband our best
shot. We try to pick up tips here and there from an occasional sermon at

church or from an article we find in an in-flight magazine on our way back home from a business trip. We tend to rely too heavily on instinct formed over the years by observation. We spent years observing how George treated Gracie, how Ozzie treated Harriet, how Mike and Carol Brady made their second marriages work with six kids in tow or, more recently, how Homer Simpson treats Marge and how Al Bundy treats Peg.

And we watched more carefully than we even realized as our fathers related as husbands to our mothers. That indelible impression shaped the husbands we would become perhaps more significantly than any other factor. We saw what Dad did right and what he did wrong. If he wasn't there, we carried into marriage an empty file in our memory that registers a blank screen every time we click on the icon.

This book is offered in the hope that it will stir up your thinking about what it means to be a husband. As I pass 25 years of marriage, I realize how much I am still learning about the primary responsibility God has called me to in this life. There's a lot more at stake here than a happy and fulfilling marriage. God's image and character have been entrusted into a pair of very clumsy hands.

A Husband Is . . .

This book is divided into three sections. In part one, we'll look at the necessary qualifications for being the husband God wants us to be. These qualifications seem almost self-evident until we scratch our way beneath the surface. The first qualification requires us to more fully understand our masculinity. God gave the assignment of husbanding to men, after first creating us to be ready for the task. We'll look at the unique ways that God has crafted the male of the species in preparing us for our role.

The second qualification we'll examine in part one is the ongoing process of spiritual growth. Any man can be a husband, but only a godly man can reflect the glory of God as he fills that sacred role. We'll look at how a man can cultivate godly character qualities in his life.

In part two of the book, we'll move from qualifications to the core role a man plays as a husband. Our model for how we are to fill the role of husband is Jesus Christ and His relationship with His Bride, the Church. In the same way that Christ has fulfilled the three Old Testament offices of priest, prophet and King, so will we see how God has called a husband to be priest, prophet and king in his relationship with his wife.

The final section of the book, part three, will look at what a husband does. We are called in Scripture to look again at the relationship between Christ and His Church in order to understand how we are to love our wives well. Hopefully, we can gain fresh insight into a subject that is inexhaustible, so that we "may be able to comprehend with all the saints what is the breadth and length and height and depth, and to know the love of Christ which surpasses knowledge, that you may be filled up to all the fullness of God" (Eph. 3:18-19).

We'll see how a husband shows his love for his wife by giving himself up for her (see Eph. 5:25). We'll look at the sanctifying role a husband can play in his wife's life, and what it means for him to keep his bride without spot or blemish. And we'll look deeply at the call for a husband to nourish and cherish his bride.

If you're not yet a husband, I hope this book can reorient your thinking about the role to which God may one day call you. If you have already accepted the sacred position as husband to your wife, your assignment is to do some honest self-evaluation and soul-searching. I believe that God wants to call each of us back to the biblical standard for how to live out the assignment of a lifetime—the awesome honor of being called a husband.

PART ONE

THE QUALIFICATIONS OF A CHRISTIAN HUSBAND

CHAPTER 1

MANHOOD
REDEFINED

Here's an exercise for you. Lay your hand—either one—palm down on a table in front of you. With your fingers together, extend the tips of your fingers as far as you can. Now look at the pointer finger and the ring finger. Which one is longer?

If you are a man, I can predict with a high degree of certainty which finger wins the contest. In almost every case, it's the ring finger on a man's hand that will extend a few millimeters beyond the outstretched pointer.

The next time you're with your wife or with a female acquaintance, ask her to do the same exercise. You will find that with women the opposite is almost always true. A woman's first finger is usually just a little longer than her third finger.

Behind that seemingly trivial observation about men's and women's fingers is hidden a profound truth. That subtle distinction between the sexes quietly speaks volumes about what makes a man a man. And before he can understand how to be a husband, a man has got to wrestle with the more fundamental issue: What defines his masculinity?

Over the past 10 years, the growing men's movement, both in the culture and in the Church, has spawned a great deal of discussion about the essence of masculinity. Too often writers have attempted to define masculinity on the basis of function. They have suggested that what defines a man is the responsible execution of male roles. For example, a man is defined by his role as a godly husband or a godly father, or by his integrity in the workplace.

This is a little like defining a lawn mower as "a machine that cuts grass, which may be accurate, but it's incomplete. Lots of machines can cut grass—from scissors to hedge trimmers. I believe if we want to really understand what a man is, we have to look beyond function to design.

In the early 1990s, Robert Hicks studied the six Hebrew words for man: *Adam* (a human creature), *zakar* (a male), *gibbor* (a warrior), *enosh* (a weak or feeble man), *ish* (a husband) and *zaken* (an old or bearded man). Hicks concluded that each word embodied the defining characteristics of a man at various stages in his life, moving from basic biology to spiritual wisdom and maturity. Every man's journey, Hicks suggested, will move him from one stage to the next, with the goal of becoming a *zaken*—a man marked by godly wisdom.

Since its release, Hicks's book *The Masculine Journey* has been criticized for reading more into the meaning of each of those Hebrew words than God intended, and for attempting to fit the square peg conclusions of the secular men's movement into a round biblical hole. Still, Hicks's book offers some helpful insights into the nature of masculinity.

Stu Weber, a pastor from the Portland area, went to what he calls "the headwaters" of masculinity—Genesis 2—and found in pre-Fall Adam four masculine characteristics. Weber says every man has in himself something of a king, a warrior, a mentor and a friend, resident in the masculine soul from the first moments of creation and implanted there by the designer. Those four "pillars," according to his book *Tender Warrior* (and later in the book *The Four Pillars of a Man's Heart*), give men a road map for biblical masculinity.

At the same time, pastor and author Robert Lewis has suggested that the essence of masculinity can be found in comparing the failed first Adam with the triumphant second Adam, the Lord Jesus Christ. In juxtaposing the two, Lewis offers men a helpful understanding of what he calls "authentic manhood."[1] Real men, according to Lewis, reject passivity, accept responsibility, lead courageously and expect the greater, eternal reward. Lewis rightly asserts that the mantle of leadership laid on men is distorted by the Fall in one of two ways: either a man is a selfish, abusive dictator or, more often, he is a passive follower who has surrendered his leadership responsibility to the women around him. Original sin, Lewis asserts, had less to do with Eve taking the serpent's fruit than it did with the silence of Adam, who was apparently standing next to his wife when the forbidden fruit was offered (see Gen. 3:6).

Hicks, Weber, Lewis and others have helped take us back to the beginning in our attempt to understand masculinity biblically. While a number of passages and verses give us an understanding of what God calls men *to do*, the Bible offers very little help in showing us *how* God uniquely created men as men.

As I'll suggest later in this chapter, I believe the master designer specially crafted the male of the species—with our long ring fingers and all—to fulfill the assignment He has for us. We can understand better what makes us men by seeing how we have been created. Before we can understand how we are to function, especially as husbands, we need to more thoroughly examine the design.

Masculine Confusion

My son Jimmy and I were on a bike ride together right before his seventh birthday when I decided to steer our conversation in a significant direction.

"Jimmy," I asked him, "what's the difference between a man and a woman?"

Jimmy got a shy grin on his face as he looked around to see who might be listening nearby. Without looking at me, he shifted his eyes and said, "You know, Dad."

I chuckled and said, "That's right, I do know. I want to see if you know."

Jimmy nervously glanced from side to side again before he blurted out his two-word answer to my question.

"Private parts," he said.

"That's right!" I told him, affirming his understanding of a concept that must have appeared obvious to him. "God made boys and girls with different private parts. What else makes men different from women?"

This time the wheels started whirring in his little mind. Beyond the obvious it was clear Jimmy had not done a lot of deep thinking about the differences between the sexes. If Jimmy was going to come up with any differences beyond "private parts," it appeared he was going to need some help.

Even as adults, men today remain confused about their own sense of what it means to be a man. For years we assumed we would someday intrinsically understand the mystery of our own masculinity. We presumed that the nature of manhood was one of those self-evident truths that would eventually dawn on the consciousness of all young boys as they began to emerge as men. No formal instruction was necessary. It would just happen.

The problem is, it isn't "just happening" today. Earlier in history, society seemed to reinforce what the Bible teaches about responsible masculinity. But in recent years a cacophony of voices has emerged, calling men to define their manhood around any number of ideas. The cultural reinforcements have not only broken down but are sending uncertain signals to young men. Confusing messages from all directions make it difficult for men to understand and embrace what it really means to be a man.

Our Fathers

For better or worse, no one has shaped our understanding of our own masculinity more than our fathers. We are marked for life by their lives, their models and their instructions—or by their absence.

As boys grow up, they begin to wrestle with what it means to be a man. Most never realize the depth or nature of the questions they subconsciously ask themselves. Young men almost automatically begin to mimic whatever they observe that seems like real masculinity to them. They search for a picture of manhood, and for most, the dominant image is that of their own father. By their active example, or even by their absence, fathers are shaping and defining masculinity for their sons. Many of those defining messages create a distorted picture of manhood for the young observers.

Ever since the early 1900s, boys have grown up in female-dominated homes as the industrial revolution brought profound change to American production. Men were moving from the fields to the factory, where they worked alongside other men six days a week, often 10 to 12 hours a day, providing for their families. The message for young boys was simple: manhood was defined in the marketplace.

No longer does a son grow up working side by side with his dad to bring in the harvest or to hunt for food for the family. A boy's most natural, most powerful definition of manhood leaves the house in the morning and comes back weary at the end of the day. From what a boy sees, a man's chief assignment—the thing that defines him as a man—is his ability to provide material goods for his family.

Boys who lived through the Great Depression watching their own fathers struggle to make ends meet learned a similar lesson. Those difficult economic conditions forced men to be single-minded in their quest to meet their family's basic needs. Times were desperate and other responsibilities were set aside. But even as economic conditions improved, a new generation of men had grown up knowing only one task as husbands and fathers—to provide for their families. What had been a fight for survival during the Great Depression evolved into a quest for prosperity in later years. Over time, that which had once been considered only part of a husband's responsibility became his sole responsibility.

What is the confusing message? Being a man means being a success in the marketplace. Period. End of discussion.

This new cultural order has pressed fathers away from the role the Scriptures assume they will play in raising their sons. Throughout the book of Proverbs sons are told to listen to the instruction and training of their fathers (see 4:1; 6:20; 23:22). Today fathers have neglected the biblical admonition to raise children "in the discipline and instruction of the Lord" (Eph. 6:4). In the process, young men who might have become disciples of their dads, and there learned the meaning of manhood, have had to look elsewhere.

At least four other sources of influence have stepped in to fill the gap created by the "provider" father: women, the media, our peers and feminism.

Women

As young men subconsciously have searched for their own masculine identity, three groups of women have come to play a significant role in shaping it. Mothers have become more involved in the process at home. Teachers, who are almost exclusively women in the lower grades, have provided role modeling and training for young boys. And female peers continue to influence the process of boys becoming men.

As fathers left the farms and headed for the factory or the office, it became obvious that someone was going to have to raise and train their sons. That role fell to Mom. She assumed the responsibility for much of the social, spiritual and physical development of her boys. How she chose to raise those sons was shaped, at least in part, by how she felt about masculinity expressed by the significant men in her life: her father, her brothers and her husband.

It is easy to understand how a young woman who has grown up with a cruel or abusive father would not want to see those same characteristics or patterns emerge in her sons. Or if her brothers or her husband have modeled sinful patterns of masculine behavior, she would want to train her sons differently.

However, some young mothers have mistakenly attempted to "correct" sinful expressions of masculine behavior by trying to make their young sons more feminine. Moms who are determined to raise nonaggressive or nonviolent sons, for example, often find themselves frustrated when two-year-old Johnny picks up a stick and starts using it as a gun. Take away the stick and Johnny uses his finger!

I don't remember the experience myself, but my mother has repeated the story enough times that I know all the details. I was two, and my next-door neighbor was about a year younger. We were playing one day in the backyard when my mom saw me push my friend to the ground and heard him start to cry. She came running.

"Bob," she scolded, "why did you push him down?"

My defense was simple. "I shot him," I told her. "He's dead, and he won't fall down!"

Boys will indeed be boys. While some have used that expression as a way to cover sinfulness, some mothers have drifted in the opposite direction. Instead of correcting sin in children, some moms and teachers have attempted to "correct" maleness in young men. Because of their own scars from the sinful men in their lives, they have mistaken certain aspects of healthy masculinity for sin. They have created a lot of gender confusion in young men by punishing and attempting to purge what might be normal male behavior.

At the same time, boys at an early age find themselves anxious for the approval and the attention of girls their own age. Boys who would otherwise behave maturely will act like monkeys or show off their strength if it will earn them an extra glance from a girl. As these boys grow, they continue to modify their behavior to attract the attention of young ladies.

Sociologist George Gilder, in his classic book *Men and Marriage*, takes this observation a step further. Gilder suggests that men are basically barbarians who must be tamed by the influence of women. The male sex drive, he says, is so powerful that in order to satisfy it men become domesticated, surrendering their freedom.[2]

Gilder holds that men of all ages will alter their own sense of masculinity to gain the affection and approval of women. At some level boys will ask the significant women in their lives, "What do you want my maleness to look like?" Then they will conform their behavior to earn the approval of those women. If a woman points a young man toward the biblical model of masculinity, she will end up with a man who can embrace his God-designed sense of masculinity. If, however, she points him away from the biblical model, she leaves him confused about his maleness, and she winds up dissatisfied with the result of her own creation.

Media

No one can deny the powerful shaping role the media have had in our culture. Prior to the advent of television, the dominant institutions shaping the next generation were the family, the community and the Church. Now the average American spends more than three hours a day watching television, and the average American household has the tube glowing almost seven hours a day. With dozens of cable channels from which to choose, young men can surf until they find the masculine role model of their choice.

When boys do not have godly fathers to model a realistic picture of manhood, they turn to television and the popular culture to find alternatives. In the '50s, John Wayne portrayed a "real" man as a warrior—tough and stoic. Today that image has evolved into the cartoonlike "superwarrior" characters portrayed by Arnold Schwarzenegger and Steven Seagal.

The media have also helped create a whole new masculine icon. The sports warrior, by virtue of his strength and raw power, seems to be the prototypical man, whether he is a Sunday-afternoon offensive lineman or a contender for the heavyweight crown. Young boys who lack the shaping guidance of a father turn to everyone from Michael Jordan to Mike Tyson for masculine identification.

TV, movies and sports give young boys a new definition of what makes a man a "real" man. It's almost the opposite of the domesticated man, who in the typical TV sitcom is an object of ridicule and scorn. That is certainly not the image of a man young boys want to emulate, so they turn to the image of the superhero. Forget being sensitive or responsible. A "real" man is powerful and reckless. He's a hero who uses force to get his way. He's a warrior.

The image of a man as a warrior appeals to us because it resonates with—and ultimately distorts something inside—every man. In one way a real man is what Stu Weber calls a "Tender Warrior." But when a man begins to see his own strength as the exclusive quality that marks his manhood, he will end up with a grotesque caricature of authentic manhood.

Peers

A young boy's definition of manhood is also being shaped in the sandbox.
Boys watch other boys to better understand what it means to be a man.

When I was in the ninth grade, I was the third-string fullback (all 140 pounds of me) on a football team that went 0-5. In spite of my size and my coordination, I had joined the team because that's what the guys I hung out with did.

For me the game was fun, whether we won or lost. But I quickly learned that playing for fun isn't a part of the cultural understanding of masculinity. In our locker room after the games, very little was heard except for the slamming of the locker doors. Outside the locker room, girlfriends waited for their defeated, angry boyfriends to emerge. They might make some vain attempt to cheer the sullen young men, but most had learned just to be quiet and let the defeated athletes brood.

From our peers, we learned that masculinity is defined and ultimately validated by victory in competition. Even today, as I play pickup games of basketball with guys my own age, the remnants of this masculine competitiveness will emerge in the middle of a "friendly game of basketball." The message from peers tends to say: All men compete, but real men win.

Feminism

In recent times, feminists have worked aggressively to redefine masculinity. As the feminist movement reshaped the American culture in the 1970s, it left in its wake an abundance of masculine confusion. While many women have united around legitimate issues such as equal pay for equal work, more radical feminists have advocated a different agenda. They have aimed to eliminate any distinction between masculinity and femininity. They have asserted that the presumed differences between men and women are artificial, imposed on our culture by years of social pressure.

Many voices have even suggested that, aside from the obvious biological differences, men and women are essentially the same. They argue that the psyche of an individual is totally detached from the biological trappings of a male or a female body. If we can only liberate people, they say, from our powerful cultural stereotypes, we will find that men and women think and behave the same.[3]

This push for gender equality has created a crisis in our corporate male psyche. Some "enlightened" elitists may have found a way to live in a constant state of gender denial. But most men, and a growing number of women, have begun to realize that pretending that men and women are the same doesn't make it so.

Still, the feminist movement has left men unsure of what is acceptable male behavior. Some women view common courtesies such as a man opening a door for a woman as pandering chauvinism.

Is it any wonder that today millions of men are asking themselves the question, "What is a real man?" Instead of being instructed from the Scriptures and discipled by their fathers, young men are watching the media exalt super warriors while their moms reward them for being peaceful. They see their peers affirming strength, power and competition, while feminists scold them for those same behaviors. When we're tough, we're told to be tender. When we're tender, other men look at us as though we're sissies. So what do we do?

The answer involves a mental realignment. Instead of looking to the world for a definition of masculinity, we need to align our thinking to what God's Word says marks a man. Instead of being conformed, we need to be transformed.

However, no definitive passage in the Bible offers us a clear portrait of masculinity. There are instructions on how to be husbands and fathers, on how to be slaves or masters, on how to function with integrity in the marketplace and on how to serve effectively in the Church, but there is no passage of Scripture that offers a clear explanation of what it means to be a man.

Or is there?

Before you turn to the next chapter, look again at your ring finger.

PointstoConsider

1. Other than the obvious physical differences, what makes a man different from a woman?

2. Before you started reading *The Christian Husband*, how would you have defined the role of the husband in a marriage?

3. What words would you use to describe your father?

4. What picture of manhood did he shape in your life? How did he see his role as a man?

5. In what ways did you benefit from his example as you grew up? In what ways was his example a detriment to you?

6. In what ways have each of the following affected your understanding of the masculine role?

- Your mother (or another significant woman in your life)
- Media
- Peers
- Feminism

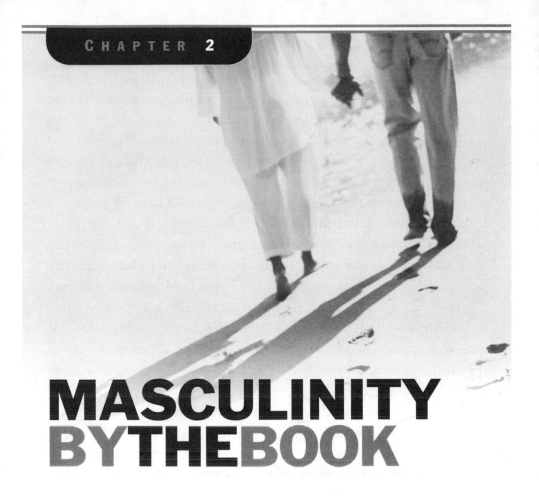

CHAPTER 2

MASCULINITY BYTHEBOOK

The differences between the sexes are the single most important fact of human society.

GEORGE GILDER, *MEN AND MARRIAGE*

I **remember laughing as I stared at the cover of the January 20, 1992, issue of *Time*.** The headline boldly proclaimed, "Why are men and women different? It isn't just upbringing. New studies show they are born that way." I read it three times just to make sure I wasn't missing something.

As my kids would say, "Duh."

The headline was both laughable and tragic. After two decades of feminist attempts to reduce the differences between men and women to a few anatomical aberrations, new scientific research on gender was making news. The latest experiments seemed to reveal that boys like trucks and girls like dolls no matter how hard we try to reorient them. In fact, give a girl a room full of trucks to play with, and she'll usually make one the daddy truck and another a mommy truck and have them talking to each other. Give a boy dolls to play with and it won't be long before Barbie is tossing hand grenades at Ken!

Before a man can understand his role as a husband, he must first understand what it means to be a man. Yet over the last 20 years men have drifted from one cultural definition to the next, unable to find the core of what marks them as men. The shifting winds of cultural preference have at one point crowned quiche-eating, sensitive Alan Alda types as "real men," only to shift to the moody, grunting Rambo as a real man's man. Movie studios bet millions of dollars each year on whether the culture is currently defining manhood as Harrison Ford or Kevin Costner.

There was no such confusion on day six of creation as God prepared to finish His work. His creation was complete, with one exception. He was about to bring to center stage in the Garden a creature unlike any of the birds, beasts and fishes he had fashioned earlier. He was ready to make His image bearer.

"Then God said, 'Let Us make man in Our image, according to Our likeness; and let them rule over the fish of the sea and over the birds of the sky and over the cattle and over all the earth, and over every creeping thing that creeps on the earth.' God created man in His own image, in the image of God He created him; male and female He created them" (Gen. 1:26-27). In his final act before declaring a day of rest, the creator fashioned two creatures who, unlike any other created being, would bear his image: a man and a woman who could reason, who could laugh and love and cry, and who could act in obedience to the will of their creator or who could rebel. To show that he had set these two apart, God gave the man and the woman dominion over the rest of His creation, naming them as coregents and calling them to subdue the earth.

While they shared the imprint of God's image, the man and the woman were created as two distinctly different beings. The biblical record is clear: He created them *male* and *female*, with what author Mike Mason calls a "mysterious, compelling combination of identity and otherness."[1] The identity gave them equal standing and equal worth before their creator; the otherness was designed by God so that they would function interdependently and, in so doing, they would reflect the nature of the Triune God. No matter how much our culture would like to erase those distinctions, there is no getting around the fact that God made men to be men and women to be women.

Much of the current discussion about what defines masculinity centers around how a man is to function in his home, in his church, in his job and in his community. We tend to define masculinity on the basis of performance, not essence. In other words, if a man does what men are supposed to do, he is a real man. While that discussion is profitable, it doesn't go far enough. Before we seek to understand the function of masculinity, we need to understand the core of masculinity. Before looking at what a man *does*, we need to understand what a man *is*.

There was a moment in time when Adam first understood that he was a man. In Genesis 2, we come to a detailed account of the creation of man and woman. God fashioned Adam from the dust of the ground, breathed life into him and placed him in the center of the Garden of Eden. He gave Adam the responsibility of tending and cultivating the garden, and also established the single requirement that he not eat from the tree in the center of the Garden, the Tree of the Knowledge of Good and Evil.

God then began the process of making a suitable helper for Adam. He directed Adam to name the animals, revealing to him in the process that while He had made mates for each of the animals, no animal was suitable to be Adam's mate. God knew it was not good for man to be alone. From eternity it had been His plan to create a woman to be Adam's companion. Now as Adam slept, God took a rib from Adam's side and fashioned it into Eve.

Adam awoke from his nap to see standing before him a creature unlike any of the animals he had named earlier in the day. He must have rubbed his eyes and stood staring at the woman God had brought to him. Here was someone more like himself than any other creature on the face of the earth. "This is bone of my bones!" Adam said. "And flesh of my flesh! She's like me! I'm not alone anymore!"

Then Adam remembered his assignment from God to name the animals. "She shall be called Woman," he said, "because she was taken out of Man."

She is a part of me, Adam must have thought. *We share something that I don't share with any other creature. Together, we share the image of God.*

Along with his realization that Eve was very much like him, Adam was also aware that God had fashioned her to be different from him. In discovering those differences, he was discovering his own uniqueness as a man. He was beginning to understand how God had crafted him with certain physical, biological and emotional distinctions. His own sense of his manhood began to emerge as he understood the ways in which he was different from Eve.

Man, the Initiator and Provider

At this point in the biblical record of creation, the author of Genesis gives the first couple some privacy. He explains that men will leave their fathers and mothers and will cleave to their wives, and that the two will become one flesh. In a modest way, Moses is telling us what happened next. God had commanded the man and woman to be fruitful and multiply, and there is no reason to believe that they wasted any time obeying his instructions!

Adam's first glimpse of what it means to be a man must have occurred almost immediately as he saw Eve for the first time. Looking at the new creature now standing naked before him, Adam must have responded as a man. A hormonal wave like he had never before experienced must have washed over him, as he felt for the first time a swelling in his loins. For the first time he was experiencing feelings that drove him to become one physically with his new bride. His first recognition of his manhood involved responding to God-given urges and enjoying a profoundly sexual experience.

If reading the last few paragraphs make you feel at all uncomfortable, you're not alone. We live in a time when the idea of a sexually aggressive man is seen as dangerous and destructive. We know too well the experience of rape, sexual violence in marriage and the link between pornography and violent behavior. We have responded to these perversions by believing that a man's sex drive is somehow perverted.

God's call for Adam and Eve to be fruitful and multiply was a welcome invitation for Adam. We have to assume that he experienced a strong desire to initiate sex as a normal and natural masculine response to the sight of a woman standing naked before him. God built that response into the design of a man and provided marriage as the sanctified place where this desire could be expressed in a healthy way.

The male sex drive is traced biologically to the androgenic hormones at work in a man's body, primarily testosterone. Sometime around the twentieth week of gestation, baby boys are literally brainwashed. The release of a small amount of testosterone from the newly formed gonads douses the baby's brain, marking him as a male. At the same time, the hypothalamus, the gland that regulates hunger and the sex drive, takes on distinctly male characteristics.

Today, evolutionary biologists go to great lengths to explain how all these biological processes are the result of natural selection. The scientific speculation on how single-celled, asexual creatures eventually became male and female is laughable. Consider the hypothesis of biologist Lynn Margulis of the University of Massachusetts at Amherst: "The evolutionary roots of egg and sperm cells can be traced back to a group of organisms known as protists that first appeared some 1.5 billion years ago." (Modern examples include protozoa, giant kelp and malaria parasites.) "During periods of starvation," Margulis conjectures, "one protist was driven to devour another. Sometimes this cannibalistic meal was incompletely digested, and the nuclei of prey and predator fused. By joining forces, the fused cells were better able to survive adversity, and because they survived, their penchant for union was passed on to their distant descendants."[2] In other words, sex was not the design of God but simply a kinder, gentler, more evolved form of cannibalism!

Adam's first urges were not to satisfy a growling stomach. The first thing that defined for Adam what it means to be a man was the hormonal rush that sparked his desire and pushed him toward Eve. Even the physical design of the sex act marked the man as the initiator and his wife as the receiver. But I doubt Adam took time to consider those implications. God had equipped Adam as a man with the hormones and physiology to be the aggressor, the initiator and the leader.

He also had set the man apart to be a provider. At some point, Adam must have wondered why God had made him from dust and made Eve from his rib. He got his answer in Genesis 3, following the Fall, when God pronounced His curse on the serpent and on the ground.[3] The consequences of the Fall for the woman involved her relationships with her husband and children.[4] For the man, the consequences involved his laboring in the soil from which he was taken (see Gen. 3:23). By the word of His mouth, God had made everything else *ex nihilo*, out of nothing. Here He chose to use dust to create man and the man's rib to create woman. The choice of those materials was not random. It served to link the man inexorably to his role as provider and the woman to her relational role as nurturer.

Later, God reinforced these distinctions by calling the man who fails to provide for his family "worse than an unbeliever" (1 Tim. 5:8). And He instructed younger women "to love their husbands, to love their children, to be sensible, pure, workers at home, kind, being subject to their own husbands, so that the word of God will not be dishonored" (Titus 2:4-5). In doing so, God called men and women to the roles He designed them to live.

Taking sexual initiative and providing for a family only define a part of what it means to be a man. These functions do not constitute the entire essence of masculinity. As we continue to explore the differences between men and women, we gain more insight into the master's design. We may not understand why God made a man's ring finger longer than his pointer and a woman's pointer longer than her ring finger, but we realize His attention to specific detail in the intricate physiological and biological differences between the sexes. While there is some mystery in those subtle differences, the more obvious distinctions provide us with a clearer sense of how masculine function is to follow design.

Vive la Différence!

When I was five, I had a friend from down the street who came over to play at our house. Her name was Dulcie, and I liked playing with her because when we played Superman or Pippi Longstocking, she would always let me be the hero. At that age, I didn't realize Pippi was a girl or Superman was a boy. It didn't matter. Heroes were heroes.

One night right before dinner, I asked my mom if my friend Dulcie could spend the night at our house. When she said no, I asked the inevitable question "Why?" Mom fumbled for words explaining that girls don't sleep over at boys' houses and that boys don't sleep over at girls' houses. Again, I wanted to know why. I don't remember how she responded when I persisted. I only remember that it didn't make any sense to me at age five. In the same way that heroes were heroes, regardless of gender, playmates were playmates, and it didn't matter to me if they were boys or girls.

By the fifth grade, though, gender differences began to matter. I still liked playing soccer or wrestling with Tommy or Steve, but I also liked spending time on the other side of the playground with Lisa. Often during recess, while others played foursquare, I would just sit and talk to Lisa. After those times, I found myself going back to class with a funny, warm feeling. I was beginning to experience the magnetic pull of womanhood. There was a difference between playing around with the guys and spending time with a girl—a big difference.

I had no idea how very different boys and girls really were. Nor did I realize that over the next few years with the onset of puberty, those differences would become more and more pronounced. My body was about to become a testosterone-manufacturing plant, pumping out 10 to 20 times more androgens than a girl's body. I was about to become taller, stronger and faster than Lisa.

Meanwhile, Lisa's body would be changing too. Her own hormones would enlarge her breasts and begin her body's 40-year cycle of ovulation, preparing itself for the possibility of motherhood. George Gilder notes that the change in an adolescent girl's body is markedly different from the experience of an adolescent boy. Her body evolves gently toward womanhood. His launches an insurrection![5]

Again, the master designer has built into His creation structural elements that make it obvious why husbands and wives play very different, complementary roles when they are married.[6]

For example, a man's basal metabolic rate is about 10 percent higher than a woman's. As a result, while boys convert energy into muscle, girls convert the same energy into fat. At 18, the average woman will have twice the body fat of her male counterpart. Boys will have stronger bones, tendons and ligaments, allowing them to do heavier work. Meanwhile, the additional body fat in a young woman's body will make it easier for her to conceive and bear children.

Men will, in general, heal more quickly from cuts and bruises. Our blood clots faster. We also have fewer sensory nerve endings in our skin and a higher tolerance to what is known as peripheral pain. Meanwhile, women can fight infection better than men. A woman's body produces more antibodies faster than a man's body. She will have fewer viral infections, and the ones she does experience will not last as long. Her body will serve her well as she raises her children in a social environment where communicable diseases spread quickly. A man's wound-healing system, on the other hand, makes him better prepared for more physical labor.

While there has been much debate about whether women should serve in combat, biology seems to point clearly to the masculine responsibility as protector. Our bodies are made for the role. In the midst of the debate, even *Newsweek* magazine had to acknowledge the differences. "On average, women are five inches shorter than men and have half the upper body strength. Female recruits are injured at twice the rate of male grunts. Because of their lighter skeletons, women are particularly plagued by stress fractures. As many as 30 percent of female Army colonels have some kind of permanent orthopedic condition; only 7 percent of male colonels do."[7]

As Dennis Rainey, the host of *FamilyLife Today*, likes to point out, we all seem to know intuitively that a man is designed to face danger, be courageous and protect the women around him. Imagine lying in bed late at night and hearing a noise downstairs. What husband would, in good conscience, nudge his wife and say, "I'm scared. You go?"

In fact, George Gilder says that men have an innate need to be warriors. In cultures where men no longer need to be hunters or warriors to provide food or protect their families, men often continue to hunt and participate in war games. He notes that among the Kalahari Bushmen, women provide most of the food for the tribe, while the men continue, without much luck, to hunt giraffes.[8]

The lists of biological, physiological and psychological differences between men and women have filled books and prompted tens of thousands of research projects. Gilder sums them up by saying that "man is rendered more aggressive, exploratory, volatile, competitive and dominant, more visual, abstract and impulsive, more muscular, appetitive and tall. He is less nurturant, moral, domestic, durable, healthy and dependable, less balanced, and less close to the ground. . . . Most of these propensities are substantiated by a large amount of cross-cultural material, combined with a growing body of physiological—particularly neuroendocrinological—data."[9]

We are men because God made us men. Our creator established what it means to be masculine when He created us. We have been equipped biologically to be the kind of men He intended.

That same biological predisposition, now tainted by sin, has given way to all kinds of abuses and much of today's masculine confusion. As men have expressed their masculinity in sinful ways, we have responded by demonizing masculinity rather than its sinful expression. The Bible catalogs how men in the last days "will be lovers of self, lovers of money, boastful, arrogant, revilers, disobedient to parents, ungrateful, unholy, unloving, irreconcilable, malicious gossips, without self-control, brutal, haters of good, treacherous, reckless, conceited, lovers of pleasure rather than lovers of God, holding to a form of godliness, although they have denied its power" (2 Tim. 3:2-5).

That's a good picture of manhood run amok. Apart from God's redemption and the sanctifying work of the Holy Spirit, a man will use his unique, God-given design for ignoble purposes. In fact, unredeemed masculinity is like a volatile explosive in the hands of a chimp! The feminist agenda of the last 30 years has been, in large measure, a response to unbiblical expressions of masculinity.

In Closing

To qualify as a husband, a man must be more than just a man. He's got to be a godly man—a man who fears God, who leads a spiritually disciplined life and who is marked by a masculine expression of godly character. He has to be more than a man's man—he has to be God's man. In the next chapter, we'll examine what makes a man godly.

PointstoConsider

1. Read Genesis 1:26-28.

- What is significant about the statement, "male and female He [God] created them"?
- What is significant about the fact that both man and woman are made in God's image?
- Why do you think one of God's first commands was for Adam and Eve to be "fruitful and multiply"?

2. Read Genesis 2:7 and 2:18-23. Why did God create Adam from the dust and then form Eve from Adam's rib?

3. Why is it important for us to realize that taking sexual initiative and providing for a family only define part of what it means to be a man? What else is involved?

4. How has God spoken to you as you have read this chapter? How can you apply these biblical truths to your life?

CHAPTER 3

COURAGEAND FEAR

I noticed her for the first time in February of 1975. The event is freeze-framed in my mind. She was dressed in blue jeans and a red T-shirt with "Arkansas Razorbacks" printed across the front. And, of course, there was the smile—the crooked, impish smile that betrayed her playfulness, her quick wit and her spunk. If the word "smitten" had not existed, it would at that moment have been invented. I was attracted and intrigued. The pursuit had begun.

Four weeks to the day from that first encounter, I found myself walking across campus with her alone, talking—getting to know her thoughts, catching a glimpse behind the smile, absorbing every word and cataloging every random bit of data. Knowledge is power, and I knew a successful pursuit would require information. It was time to move to risky territory in our conversation.

"Were there particular guys you dated at Arkansas?"

She told me about David, the handsome Air Force recruit. It sounded from the way she described it that she floated in and out of his radar screen from time to time. He was dating others.

She also mentioned James, the big, strong guy she had met at a Bible study on campus. He sounded like the more focused pursuer, the more formidable foe.

The enemy, I thought to myself. Were these two guys viable competition? What did they have that I didn't?

"James and I kind of quit going out at the end of last semester," she revealed.

Yes! One down.

"We still write to each other from time to time."

Whoops. Premature enthusiasm. He may have been on the sidelines, but he was not, apparently, completely out of the game.

"Why did the two of you quit dating?" I asked. What was the fatal flaw? How had he let this beauty slip through his hands?

As long as I live, I'll never forget her answer to that question. Without hesitation, the woman I would eventually woo and win, said, "He just didn't lead the relationship spiritually."

Like a student learning a new technical term in algebra or physics, I filed away the four words she had used to describe a concept that was completely foreign to me. The reason James was temporarily out of the running for Mary Ann's affection was because of something she described as "leading the relationship spiritually."

Instantly, I realized two things: (1) this idea of spiritual leadership in a relationship was important to this woman I hoped to win; and (2) I didn't have a clue what she meant by spiritual leadership.

If I'm going to stand a chance with this wonderful woman, I thought to myself, *I'd better figure out what it means.*

The qualifications for being a husband are simple but not easy. A man has to be a man, not just physically, but in the full sense of the word. And a man has to be godly.

In their book *The Silence of Adam*, Larry Crabb, Don Hudson and Al Andrews point to the interconnectedness between godliness and masculinity:

The only way to be manly is first to be godly. In our day, men are looking for their manhood more than they are seeking God. Too many men make the mistake of studying masculinity and trying to practice what they learn without paying enough attention to their relationship with God.[1]

Understanding the unique way in which you were created doesn't make you fully a man. Getting married and having a family doesn't make you a man. Success in the marketplace, great wealth and power, and the honor and praise of the culture are not the measure of real masculinity. To be fully a man, you must commit yourself to the pursuit of godliness.

It's almost a paradox, the idea of a godly man. Not because a man is incapable of godliness, but because of what is at the root of the idea of godliness in the Scriptures. We are called to live out our masculinity with courage and in fear.

The Beginning of Godliness

King Solomon wanted for his son what most fathers want for their boys. He wanted him to be successful. He wanted him to be happy. He wished for long life for his boy. He wanted him to know God and to walk with Him. He wanted his son to be a godly man.

Over time Solomon passed along to his son a treasury of wisdom that we know today as the book of Proverbs. Filled with practical counsel on everything from personal finances to the kind of woman a man should look for as a wife, Proverbs rings with a central theme. A godly life, according to Solomon, begins with wisdom. And the beginning of wisdom is the fear of the Lord:

- "The fear of the LORD is the beginning of knowledge; fools despise wisdom and instruction" (1:7).
- "Do not be wise in your own eyes; fear the LORD and turn away from evil" (3:7).
- "The fear of the LORD is the beginning of wisdom, and the knowledge of the Holy One is understanding" (9:10).

- "The fear of the LORD prolongs life, but the years of the wicked will be shortened" (10:27).
- "In the fear of the LORD there is strong confidence, and his children will have refuge" (14:26).
- "The fear of the LORD is a fountain of life, that one may avoid the snares of death" (v. 27).
- "The fear of the LORD leads to life, so that one may sleep satisfied, untouched by evil" (19:23).

In the more than 900 verses passed down from Solomon to his son, there is nowhere found a command to love God. However, Solomon implores this young man to seek wisdom and understanding over and over again, verse after verse. The man who was blessed by God with the gift of wisdom urges his son to seek the same gift.

It begins, Solomon says, in learning to fear the Lord.

It's not unusual to hear a casual observer of Christianity make a statement such as "I don't care much for the God of the Old Testament, the angry, jealous, warlike God who wants people to fear Him. I like the God of the New Testament, the God of love."

People who make statements like that fail to realize a significant truth found in the Bible. The God of the Old Testament and the God of the New Testament are the same God! There was no transfer of power from one God to the next just before the birth of Christ. God did not have an attitude adjustment during the intertestamental period, where he "mellowed out." The same God who rained fire on Sodom and who brought a flood that destroyed everyone except Noah and his family is the God who came to earth in human flesh, teaching men to love their enemies and to pray for their persecutors.

To those who like the portrait of God found in the pages of the New Testament better than the picture they see in the Old Testament, I would suggest that the only way to know the God of love is to begin by fearing Him. The pathway to the knowledge of God begins with a holy fear. In fact, if a man claims to know and love God, and he has not first learned what it means to fear him, I would submit that he doesn't really understand what love is all about.

What Does It Mean to Fear God?

Most of the time when we speak of the "fear of the Lord," we are quick to explain that the word "fear" doesn't mean "to be in terror or to dread"; it means rather that we are "to have a reverential respect" for God.

While the idea of a deep respect is part of what it means to fear God, this definition does not do justice to the fear that would rise up in the hearts of the descendants of Abraham when they considered the works of Yahweh. They had seen the Lord of hosts bring His angelic armies to destroy their enemies (see 2 Kings 6:15-17; 19:35). They had watched in awe as God brought judgment on men within their own tribe—men like Achan, who had disobeyed God at Ai and kept back some of the spoils of battle for himself. God had sentenced Achan and his family to death by stoning (see Josh. 7).

Or consider Uzzah, the soldier selected for the high honor of guarding the Ark of the Covenant as it was carried into Jerusalem during the time of David. The Israelites had seen Yahweh strike him dead for attempting to keep the Ark from falling to the ground. He had reached over and touched it in violation of God's command and instantly died (see 2 Sam. 6:1-7).

The nation of Israel would learn over and over again that their God—Yahweh—is a God to be feared.

Do I Fear God, or Am I Just Afraid of Him?

There is a difference, however, between fearing God and being afraid. In fact, Moses, after receiving the Ten Commandments from God, appeared before the Israelites, who were filled with fear:

> Moses said to the people, "Do not be afraid; for God has come in order to test you, and in order that the fear of Him may remain with you, so that you may not sin" (Exod. 20:20).

"There is a fear that is slavish," writes John Piper, "that drives us away from God, and there is a fear that is sweet and draws us to God. . . . God means for His power and holiness to kindle fear in us, not to drive us from Him, but to drive us to Him. His anger is against those who forsake Him and love other things more."²

As a young boy, I remember watching *The Wizard of Oz* each year on television. Before the dawn of the VCR, the annual airing of the 1939 classic was a family event.

Etched in my mind is the scene where Dorothy, the Tin Man, the Scarecrow and the Cowardly Lion are ushered into the presence of "the great and powerful Oz." Barely able to move forward, they face the huge, disembodied head glowing through the smoke and hear his booming voice reverberate as he demands to know what has brought them to see him. "I am the great and powerful Oz!" he thunders as the four companions quake in his presence.

Dorothy and her friends had more than just a reverential awe of the Wizard. They trembled before him. Compare the way they approached the throne of a phony wizard with the way most Christians today come before the throne of grace. We have lost our sense of what it means to fear the Lord.

In his book *One Home at a Time*, Dennis Rainey says:

> God is not feared today. In fact, He is mocked by our immorality, our treatment of unborn human life, our broken commitments, and the selfish, "me-first" attitude that characterizes so much of what we do. Even in the Christian community, we are strangely silent about the fear of God. There is little teaching on judgment for sin, and the place of eternal torment called hell. We haven't rejected God. But we have conveniently recreated Him in our image. We have reduced the Almighty to our level.³

Today there is such an emphasis on God's great love for us that we have forgotten what it means to fear Him. We don't see Him as a consuming fire but as a kindly grandfather who chides us when we are mischievous, always with a twinkle in His eye and only a faint sternness in His voice. Don McCullough writes, "We prefer to imagine a deity who happily lets bygones be bygones, who winks at failures and pats us on the back to build our self-esteem. But according to Scripture, 'God is love.' And love devoid of judgment is only watered down kindness."⁴

Do I Respect and Trust God?

I wonder if those who say they love God but who have not learned what it means to fear Him really understand what they are talking about. I speak from experience. During my late teens and early 20s, I considered myself a Christian. I went to church regularly during college while most of my fellow classmates slept in. I went to Bible studies, worked in an outreach ministry to high school students and spent most of my time in the company of other Christians. I had prayed the prayer, I could talk the talk, and I didn't smoke, drink or do drugs. I was the all-American Christian college student.

Things changed, though, during the summer between my sophomore and junior years. I was part of a weekly Bible study with a group of friends. We met to discuss the Scriptures and to enjoy one another's company.

Following one of the sessions, one of the guys in the group asked me if we could meet during the week. I agreed, wondering what his agenda might be, thinking to myself that he must want me to explain some issue from the Scriptures to him.

As we sat in his apartment one afternoon a few days later, he gently but firmly said to me, "I don't think you get it. You don't understand the depth of your sin, and I don't think you understand the grace of God in offering you His gift of salvation. He didn't die on the Cross just to give your life purpose and meaning. You were His sworn enemy, and He came to rescue you from the punishment in hell that you deserve!"

His words stung my soul that afternoon. I left his apartment feeling weak in the knees. Most of the gospel presentations I had heard had focused on a kind, loving God who wanted me to have an abundant life. I had heard countless times about a God who wanted to have a relationship with me, who would show me His plan for my life and who would let me go to heaven when I die.

Lutheran theologian Dr. Rod Rosenbladt said, "If your doctrine of sin is not as deep as the text of Scripture, you probably do not have a real Savior on the cross!" That afternoon, for the first time in my life, I found myself humbled before an almighty God who had chosen by His grace to spare my life and adopt me into His family. Instead of giving me what I deserve—eternal punishment—He chose to grant me the gift of eternal life with Him.

For love to exist in any relationship, there must first be respect and trust. Anything we call "love" that does not have a foundation of respect and trust is just a bunch of sloppy sentiment.

Jesus warned His disciples:

> Not everyone who says to Me, "Lord, Lord," will enter the kingdom of heaven, but he who does the will of My Father who is in heaven will enter. Many will say to Me on that day, "Lord, Lord, did we not prophesy in Your name, and in Your name cast out demons, and in Your name perform many miracles?" And then I will declare to them, "I never knew you; depart from Me, you who practice lawlessness" (Matt. 7:21-23).

If your love for Christ is not firmly founded on the fear of God, you should ask yourself whether your faith is truly saving faith. "The fear of the LORD is the beginning of wisdom, and the knowledge of the Holy One is understanding" (Prov. 9:10).

"Act Like Men"

Paradoxically, our fear of God ought to be the basis of great courage in us. As men who fear God, we learn that we are not to fear other men. "Do not fear those who kill the body but are unable to kill the soul," Jesus taught, "but rather fear Him who is able to destroy both soul and body in hell" (Matt. 10:28). Our fear of God should produce boldness in the face of opposition from men.

Tucked away at the end of his letter to the Church at Corinth, the apostle Paul gives a solemn charge to those men who are leaders of the Church. "Be on the alert," he writes, "stand firm in the faith, act like men, be strong. Let all that you do be done in love" (1 Cor. 16:13-14). In those five simple statements, he calls the men who lead God's Church to a foundational quality of masculine godliness. He calls them to be men of courage.

In fact, some translations of the Bible take the clause "act like men" (*andrizesthe* in Greek) and translate it "be courageous." Earlier, Paul had chastised the Corinthians for acting like babies. "I gave you milk to drink, not solid food," he wrote, "for you were not yet able to receive it. Indeed, even now you are not yet able" (3:2). By the end of his epistle, Paul exhorts his readers to act like men. The expression "act like men" is a call to maturity, to conviction and to courage.

A Call to Courage

In the face of danger, in the face of adversity, a man is to respond in courage. If a husband is going to fulfill his calling to love and lead his wife, he is going to need to draw on his courage and his convictions. He will have to stay alert to spiritual and physical danger. He will have to stand firm in the faith and lovingly lead his wife to stand firm with him. He will have to be courageous and act like a man.

Frederica Matthewes-Green talked about men and courage in an essay that aired on *National Public Radio*. "It's part of the guy job description," she said. "Whenever there's danger, any man is expected to protect any woman at any cost. This is true no matter who she is; it's not an honor awarded only to his wife or daughter.

"We hear plenty of persistent, and sometimes justified, complaining that women get a raw deal in life, that men get all the breaks. But we forget one thing guys do for us, without thinking, over and over again. It's something we expect from them; we may even take it for granted. We expect them to risk their lives."[5]

While we may have the courage to protect our wives from imminent danger, are we men enough to step out on the courage of our convictions to protect our wives from spiritual danger? Are we alert enough as men even to know when spiritual danger is present?

Today, men may still act instinctively to protect a woman from harm. What is lacking, however, is the moral courage needed to lead and protect a wife from those things that would lead her into temptation—"the lust of the flesh and the lust of the eyes and the boastful pride of life" (1 John 2:16). Too often we lack that kind of courage and leadership because we are vulnerable to the same temptations. Taking a courageous stand in the face of moral temptation requires that we first be willing to deal with our own sinful tendencies in those areas.

Often our desire to please our wife or to keep the peace in our relationship will cause us to compromise. While we are never to be inconsiderate of our wife's feelings or her desires, we are to courageously follow God. There will be times when she will not like our courage or our convictions. She may choose to withhold affection or lash out in anger. There will be conflict. In those moments, you will think to yourself, *Surely God wants us to be at peace*, and you may be tempted to weaken. The courageous man will stand firm.

When the Word of God calls us to courage, it anticipates the likelihood that we will abuse that call, so Paul writes, "Let all that you do be done in love" (1 Cor. 16:14) to remind us that our courage must always be lived out in the power of the Holy Spirit. Courage without love is nothing more than bullying. Leadership without compassion is tyranny. Many of the abuses of masculinity that we have seen throughout the years have come from men who have attempted to "act like men" without doing all that they do in love.

Return to Chivalry

Just after midnight on April 15, 1912, in the middle of the North Atlantic, hundreds of men faced the challenge of going against their natural instinct for self-preservation and laid down their lives for their women and their children. As they tucked their wives and children safely in one of the few lifeboats on board the *Titanic*, those men bravely stepped back, waved goodbye to their families and waited to die.

From that time until today, the sinking of the *Titanic* has captured the curiosity and imagination of millions who read Walter Lord's 1952 book *A Night to Remember* or who viewed James Cameron's 1997 movie *Titanic*. The sinking of the great ship is a landmark historical event, seared on our collective consciousness. Historians and sociologists have discussed at length the significance of the event. Some have seen it as a wake-up call to those who had begun to embrace the arrogance of industrial optimism, believing that man was indeed invincible on the heels of the industrial revolution. Others have called the *Titanic* a microcosm of man's ongoing class struggle, as the passengers in steerage were kept below while the first-class passengers boarded the lifeboats.

Woven in between those subplots, almost indistinguishable, are the heroism and chivalry of the men who did what the Scriptures exhort husbands to do. Douglas Phillips comments:

> With only a few exceptions, *Titanic's* men willingly gave up their seats on lifeboats for others, thus exemplifying the Bible verse: "Greater love hath no man than he lay down his life for another." The most poignant examples came from the many incidents in which families were split up. Husbands literally looked into the eyes of their wives and children, whispered tender last words, and lowered their families into lifeboats with the full realization that they would never see them again. Thus, one of *Titanic's* greatest ironies is that she became a symbol of duty and faith.[6]

The men on board the *Titanic* responded to catastrophe with courage and love. The lifeboats were the place for women and children. "For 1,000 years this principle has guided Western civilization. Simply stated, that principle is this—the groom dies for the bride, the strong suffer for the weak, and the highest expression of love is to give your life for another. This is the true meaning of biblical patriarchy. The men aboard the *Titanic* recognized their duty because they had been raised in a culture that implicitly embraced such notions. Only by returning to these foundations can we ever hope to live in a society in which men will make the self-conscious decision to die so that women and children may live."[7]

In Closing

In order to live as we were designed to live, we must be in pursuit not simply of manhood but of godly masculinity. That begins by being men who are rightly related to God, who understand what it means to fear Him and who respond to that fear by being alert, standing firm in the faith and being men of courage.

PointstoConsider

1. Earlier in the chapter, I wrote:

> Understanding the unique way in which you were created doesn't make you fully a man. Getting married and having a family doesn't make you a man. Success in the marketplace, great wealth and power, and the honor and praise of the culture are not the measure of real masculinity. To be fully a man, you must commit yourself to the pursuit of godliness.

How do you respond to that statement?

2. To fear God means to have a reverential respect for Him. What do the following verses tell us about why it is important for a man to fear God?

- Proverbs 3:7
- Proverbs 9:10
- Proverbs 10:27

3. What will happen to the man who does not fear God? Can you think of an example of a man who considers himself to be a Christian but does not display any fear of God? How can this be seen in his attitudes and in his actions?

4. What does 1 Corinthians 16:13 tell us about manhood?

5. In what areas do men need to show courage in their lives? In what areas do *you* need to show courage?

CHAPTER 4

A MAN AND GOD'S WORD

Any man who hopes to be a godly husband will find it necessary to understand what it means to be a man of courage who fears the Lord. He must also be committed to the goal of personal holiness. If he's not first and foremost a godly man, he'll never be the kind of husband God has called him to be. His respect and reverence for the One who has bought his life back from the slave market of sin should provide the drive and determination to live his newly redeemed life in a way that honors his creator.

A man who assumes the responsibility of being a husband makes a covenant before God to fulfill certain duties that are discussed later in this book. Many men today barely attempt to honor their commitments in marriage, yielding instead to their own selfish impulses. Even among professing Christians, many men only make a token effort to care for their brides. They are more committed to their own desires than to their scriptural obligations as husbands.

Tom and Laurie's situation is all too typical. After more than a dozen years of marriage, including the birth of three delightful, high-spirited children, their own relationship was struggling. Laurie begged for them to see a counselor, and Tom finally consented.

Six months later, Tom arrived home one evening and announced to Laurie that he couldn't continue to live a charade. He didn't love her anymore, and it was hypocrisy for them to stay together. He needed some time and some space to clear his head and figure things out.

Through her tears, Laurie watched Tom pack a suitcase with enough clothing to last a few days and then back the car out of the driveway. He never again spent a night in that home. In less than a year, his head had apparently cleared. He was now living with a young woman he had met at work, spending weekends at the beach and driving a new sports car.

Tom's frustration in his marriage had little to do with Laurie. He wanted out from under the weight of responsibilities he faced as a husband and a father. With his new girlfriend, he could spend his evenings and weekends doing what he wanted to do, instead of fixing a broken patio door or giving his children a bath. His head didn't need clearing; he simply wanted to be rid of his husbandly duties. He now had the freedom he craved, and he had been able to trade in a fairly routine sex life with his wife for something that appeared to have a little more spice.

Tom's commitment to being a husband lasted until it was no longer convenient or enjoyable. When the thrill faded, his interest waned. He lived with his obligations longer than he wanted to before setting out in search of his own happiness.

Like tens of thousands of husbands, Tom defaulted on the vow he made before God, exchanging it for a vow to live for himself. He showed no fear of God in reneging on the oath he had sworn to love, honor and cherish "till death us do part." Instead of acting like a man, he cowardly chose to run from his responsibilities.

Tom may not be the average Christian husband, but his story is all too common in the community of faith. His casual commitment to his responsibilities betrays a lack of commitment to living a spiritually-disciplined life.

Tom's response to his marital dissatisfaction was a little more reckless and rebellious than Ben's. Married to Patti for 25 years, Ben has not only stayed with his wife but has remained faithful to her as well, something he reminds himself of with a sense of pride and accomplishment. With their fourth child about to finish high school and their oldest daughter married with two girls of her own, Ben and Patti enjoy a reputation in the community as a successful, happily married couple.

Very few people know the real story.

Ben traces it back to when Julie, their oldest, was born. He was at a point in his career where things were accelerating. The company was growing and he was one of its rising stars in sales. It meant some long hours, some extra travel and some sacrifices, but the money was good, and soon Ben and Patti might be able to buy the house they wanted with a bigger backyard and an extra bedroom.

Besides, Ben loved the excitement and the challenges he faced at work. His boss routinely commented on his excellent work. His coworkers admired him. It pleased him that every few months a "headhunter" would call and ask if he'd like to meet to discuss a job with a competing company.

Meanwhile, Patti was busy with the new demands of motherhood. Ben's job had made it possible for her to leave her career and be at home with the kids. She loved being a mom and poured herself into the task. She was homeroom mother at school, drove the kids on field trips and taxied them back and forth to soccer games. She was even able to redecorate the new house, getting it just the way she wanted it.

Both Ben and Patti noticed from time to time that their relationship seemed a little stale, yet they ignored the feelings and pressed on. What did they have to complain about? Ben had a great job and was making a good living. Patti had a beautiful house and four well-behaved children who were doing well in school. Those things helped cover the growing sense of isolation that had crept into their marriage.

Over time that sense of isolation bubbled to the surface. Ben was frustrated by the fact that Patti and he only had sex once or twice a month, and when they did, she was accommodating but unresponsive. For her part, Patti would occasionally get angry about something and would let loose her pent-up frustrations. They never talked anymore. She was worried about their daughter's new boyfriend and needed Ben's help, but he was leaving for a week-long business trip—again. He had already apologized for having to be out of town on their anniversary, and she had said it was all right, but deep down she thought to herself, *If he really loved me* . . .

Now, with Julie married, Don in graduate school, Sandy in her junior year of college and Libby about to finish high school, Ben and Patti lived alone together in a big, almost empty house. Patti was taking up new hobbies to fill her time. Between the office and golf, Ben kept busy. Most nights, he would fall asleep in front of the TV before the late news was over.

The majority of Christian men do not default on their wedding vows as Tom did. Many more wind up like Ben, failing to cultivate their marriage and ending up isolated and lonely. It's obvious that Tom failed to honor his wedding vows. Ben's failure is less obvious but no less real. He failed to love, honor and cherish his wife.

A growing number of men today have fathers like Tom or Ben. They have purposed to be better husbands than their dads are. They are determined to be different and to avoid the mistakes their fathers make. Unfortunately, they're not sure exactly how to do it. Too few of these men are looking to the Scriptures for direction.

Instead, they take their cues from the culture and try to "do their part" in a marriage. They pitch in around the house, taking out the trash and cutting the grass. They bring home the bacon, or at least a share of it, toiling at their jobs. They help with the kids, giving baths and reading stories from time to time, and attend an occasional open house at school. When they measure their performance, they can usually pat themselves on the back as a "better than average" husband.

Most of these husbands have never looked seriously at what God expects from a man as a husband. Instead, they are content if their marriage somehow meets or exceeds what they see around them.

Meanwhile, God is calling us to something more than mediocrity as husbands. In an age of casual Christianity, God is calling men to gold-medal faith in Christ. Our devotion to His cause and His Kingdom should rival or exceed the intensity exhibited by the distance runners who are training for the next Olympiad. We need daily conditioning. A casual, spiritual workout or a trip to church once a week will not suffice.

Where do we begin our quest for godly character? We begin where that kind of character is defined and modeled—the Word of God.

Bible Reading

I remember several years ago attending a weekend Bible conference at our church. Although I can't remember the name of the man who spoke, or what subject he covered, one thing he said has stuck with me.

During one of his presentations, the speaker commented on his regular discipline of Bible reading. "I was 28 when I felt called into the ministry," he said. "Someone suggested to me that if I intended to make the teaching of God's Word my vocation, I ought to read it through, in its entirety, at least once or twice."

He went on. "I purposed at that point to read through the Bible at least once every year from then on. I set aside a half hour each day for Bible reading and found I had finished my first pass in about four months.

"Since that time, I've been able to make up for the years I missed. I'm 41 now, and I've read through the Bible 43 times. It has been one of the highlights of my spiritual life."

Have you thought about what it will be like someday in heaven to meet Obadiah or Nahum? These two prophets wrote two of the least-read books in the Bible. Someday in eternity, no doubt, you're going to bump into the two of them and probably ask, somewhat sheepishly, "What was your book about, anyway?"

Frankly, I've struggled with the assignment of reading the Bible from cover to cover. I hit confusing passages and want to dig in and figure it out before I move on. I labor through the genealogies in Numbers. I struggle with the significance to my life of the correct placement of the Urim and Thummin on the priestly garments in Exodus. It's hard to read a book like Amos or Micah without knowing why the prophets are so riled up.

Whether or not we find the Bible confusing, God has some pretty remarkable things to say about His Word:

God's Word provides us with divine guidance. "Your word is a lamp to my feet and a light to my path" (Ps. 119:105). We are like men on a dark path at night, trying not to stumble. God's Word is a light that directs us to safety and steers us away from danger.

God's Word helps us see our own heart more clearly. "For the word of God is living and active and sharper than any two-edged sword, and piercing as far as the division of soul and spirit, of both joints and marrow, and able to judge the thoughts and intentions of the heart" (Heb. 4:12). Even when we can't discern the motives in our own wicked heart, God's Word can judge for us.

God's Word equips us for godly living. "All Scripture is inspired by God and profitable for teaching, for reproof, for correction, for training in righteousness; so that the man of God may be adequate, equipped for every good work" (2 Tim. 3:16-17). God uses His Word to teach us, to correct us, to scold us and to make us more like Christ.

God's Word leads us to eternal life. "But these have been written so that you may believe that Jesus is the Christ, the Son of God; and that believing you may have life in His name" (John 20:31). The apostle Paul makes it clear that faith in God comes from hearing God's Word (see Rom. 10:17). Bible scholars have long agreed that a man can *know there is a God* on the basis of general revelation (such as observing God's creation), but no man can *know God* apart from special revelation (the Scriptures).

In Psalm 119, the longest of the 150 psalms in the Bible, David speaks in verse after verse about his love for God's Word. He praises God's statutes, His commandments, His laws, His judgments, His precepts, His testimonies and His ways. The longest song in the Jewish songbook is a hymn to the greatness of God's Word.

In Psalm 19:7-11, David again speaks of the value of God's Word:

> The law of the LORD is perfect, restoring the soul; the testimony of the LORD is sure, making wise the simple. The precepts of the LORD are right, rejoicing the heart; the commandment of the LORD is pure, enlightening the eyes. The fear of the LORD is clean, enduring forever; the judgments of the LORD are true; they are righteous altogether. They are more desirable than gold, yes, than much fine gold; sweeter also than honey and the drippings of the honeycomb. Moreover, by them Your servant is warned; in keeping them there is great reward.

How can we neglect that which is more desirable than gold and sweeter than honey?

God's Word is powerful! It's living and active! If you'll commit yourself to the regular discipline of reading God's Word, and seek to know the God who is revealed in its pages, He'll use it to make you a godly man.[1]

Bible Study

Among his other accomplishments, the German reformer Martin Luther translated the Bible from Latin into German, the language of his people, so that they might be able to study God's Word for themselves. When asked about his own study of Scripture, Luther said that he studied his Bible in the same way that he gathered apples. First, he shook the whole tree that the ripest might fall. Then he shook each limb, and when he had shaken each limb, he shook each branch, and after each branch, every twig. Finally, he looked under every leaf.

Tools for Study

One January, I had resolved to read through my Bible during the coming year. (I have since learned the folly of making New Year's resolutions!) On January fourth, I found myself beginning for the first time to read through the story of the life of Abraham, beginning in Genesis 12. By the time I was finished with my 15-minute Bible reading, I had followed Abraham from the land of Ur to the Promised Land; I had been introduced to the first declaration of the Abrahamic covenant; I had read about the patriarch's journey to Egypt, where he lied to the Pharaoh, telling him that his wife Sarah was really his sister; I had seen Abraham and Lot go their separate ways; and I had been introduced to the great priest Melchizedek, who came from nowhere and is never heard from again.

My mind was flooded with questions. Had the great father of the nation of Israel, the man whose faith had been reckoned as righteousness, really lied about his wife's identity? Who was the mysterious Melchizedek, and why had Abraham paid a tithe to him? What was the significance of the covenant between Abraham and God?

I couldn't go on. In fact, I spent the next few months studying and leading a small group Bible study on the life of Abraham. I didn't make it through the Bible that year, but I did learn tremendous lessons from a study of the life of the great patriarch of Israel.

Bible study can be an intimidating prospect, especially for someone who hasn't had any training. If scholars who know Greek and Hebrew spend their lives trying to understand the Scriptures, how can we expect to learn anything as we stumble through names we can't pronounce?

As believers in Christ, we are not left alone to wade through the pages of Scripture, hoping to make some sense of it all. After announcing to His disciples that He was about to be put to death, Jesus told them He would send them the Holy Spirit as their guide:

> But when He, the Spirit of truth, comes, He will guide you into all the truth; for He will not speak on His own initiative, but whatever He hears, He will speak; and He will disclose to you what is to come (John 16:13).

The indwelling Spirit of God is the One who will lead us into all truth as we study the pages of Scripture.

In addition, we have tremendous resources available to us as we seek to know God's Word. We can begin with a study Bible, such as the *NIV*

Study Bible or the *New Geneva Study Bible*, where along with the text of Scripture are helpful notes to help you understand confusing passages.[2] Bible commentaries and Bible dictionaries are designed to help us better understand God's Word. A Bible concordance is a helpful tool for those who want to better understand the meaning of specific words in Scripture. All of these tools are available at Christian bookstores or in many church or public libraries.[3]

Also, take advantage of the myriad opportunities to study the Bible. There may be Bible classes offered through your church, or you may have community-wide Bible study groups (such as Bible Study Fellowship or Precept Bible Studies) in your area. Christian radio is a wonderful source for regular Bible teaching and study. Audiocassettes of sermons can be a great asset to the student of God's Word. And, of course, every Sunday your pastor should be helping you learn and grow in your understanding of the Bible and its application to everyday life.

Tips for Study

During the first five years of our marriage, I worked as a salesman, making calls on clients throughout the city. It was not unusual for me to spend an hour or two in the car each day, in addition to my 30-minute commute to and from work. My daily drive to the office was perfectly timed so that I could hear John MacArthur's daily radio program, *Grace to You*, as I faced the rush hour. Throughout the rest of the day, I listened to audiocassette messages from a wide array of Bible teachers as I drove from one appointment to another.

That period in my life was marked by tremendous spiritual growth as I learned principles from God's Word. I'm afraid I may have even rushed a sales call or two because I was anxious to continue listening to a particularly interesting audiocassette! I was able to renew my mind (see Rom. 12:2) and make the most of my time (see Eph. 5:16) as I traveled from one business to the next.

In writing to his young protégé Timothy, the apostle Paul challenged him to "be diligent to present yourself approved to God as a workman who does not need to be ashamed, accurately handling the word of truth" (2 Tim. 2:15). A godly man is committed to being a serious student of God's Word.

Bible Meditation and Memorization

"How blessed is the man," the Bible says, **"who does not walk in the counsel of the wicked, nor stand in the path of sinners, nor sit in the seat of scoffers!** But his delight is in the law of the LORD, and in His law he meditates day and night" (Ps. 1:1-2).

The idea of meditation may stir up images of people sitting cross-legged on the floor, eyes closed, palms up, humming or chanting sounds or phrases you can't understand. You may have been taught to meditate as a technique for relaxation. The biblical idea of meditation revolves around letting your mind dwell on the truth of Scripture, the wonder of God's creation, His divine attributes and His goodness to us. Paul directs our meditation to "whatever is true, whatever is honorable, whatever is right, whatever is pure, whatever is lovely, whatever is of good repute, if there is any excellence and if anything worthy of praise, dwell on these things" (Phil. 4:8).

In addition to reading and studying the Bible, we are instructed to chew it the way a cow chews its cud. All of us have seen a cow in the field, endlessly working over a mouthful of grass like a baseball pitcher chomping his chewing gum. The trek that grass will follow through a cow's digestive system helps to illustrate how we are to meditate on the Scriptures. But be warned—this is not something you'll want to share with your wife at the breakfast table!

Biologists say that cows have four stomachs. After a cow has chewed her mouthful of grass for a time, she swallows it and sends it to the first stomach, where her digestive juices soften it up. Once it's ready, the cow brings the cud back from stomach one to her mouth, where she continues grinding the grass with her teeth, squeezing out every bit of nutritional value. Then the wad of partially digested grass is sent to stomach number two, where it continues to be partially digested, before it comes back to Bessie's mouth for further mastication. The process continues until the cud is ready to go to stomach number four before it finally passes completely through the cow's system.

When we meditate on God's Word, we chew on it the way a cow chews its food, squeezing all the meaning and understanding we can out of a particular passage. In his helpful book *Spiritual Disciplines for the Christian Life*, Don Whitney offers some suggestions on how we can meditate on God's Word:

- *Repeat it in different ways.* Read a verse several times, emphasizing a different word each time. Each time you do, think about the different understanding you have of the verse when you emphasize a different word. Whitney says it's like turning a diamond to examine every facet.
- *Rewrite it in your own words.* Think of synonyms for different words. Or imagine a friend of yours coming to you and asking, "What does this verse mean?" How would you explain it?
- *Pray through the text.* In this way, you can personalize the passage, bringing it alive and applying it to your own situation. Obviously, many of the historical or narrative passages of the Bible don't fit with this method. But the Psalms and the Epistles provide a rich source of passages that can be personalized and prayed back to God.

  As an example, consider the well-known text of Psalm 23. Listen to how it sounds when the text is restated as a prayer: "Lord, you are my shepherd. I have all I need. You make me lie down in green pastures. You lead me beside still waters. You restore my soul."

One practical and helpful way to combine Bible study and meditation is to read through several chapters of the Bible each day for 30 days. You might begin, for example, with the book of Ephesians. The repetitious reading of those six chapters of Scripture will yield a number of benefits. First, you'll become very familiar with the text as you read it over and over. You'll also find new understanding of particular passages as you read them again. By the end of the 30 days, you'll be surprised at how much you've retained from your study and how your understanding of that particular section of the Bible has increased.

God's Word also exhorts us to memorize verses or passages from the Bible. In Colossians 3:16, Paul writes, "Let the word of Christ richly dwell within you." David declares in Psalm 119:11, "Your word I have treasured in my heart, that I may not sin against You." Throughout the life of Jesus, we see Him quoting passages of the Old Testament from memory, using Scriptures to teach His followers or to confound His enemies.

Before we were married, Mary Ann and I decided to try to memorize a whole chapter of the Bible. It seemed like an exercise in futility to me. Mary Ann suggested Philippians 2, and since I knew very little about the Bible, one chapter was as good as any other chapter.

I think Mary Ann eventually made it through verse 13. I flamed out at about verse 6 or 7, but not before God had had a chance to burn into my brain the two verses I would need to have on the tip of my tongue throughout my life. Those were verses 3 and 4:

Do nothing from selfishness or empty conceit, but with humility of mind regard one another as more important than yourselves; do not merely look out for your own personal interests, but also for the interests of others.

For some reason, I was able to memorize those verses with very little effort! Still today God brings that passage to mind regularly as He exposes my selfishness and reminds me to be humble and self-sacrificing.

If memorizing verses from the Bible is difficult for you, let me suggest that you invest in music audiocassettes or CDs to listen to with your children. Our family has enjoyed listening to the *Hide 'Em in Your Heart* series (volumes 1 and 2) by Steve Green and the *G. T. and the Halo Express* tapes. The songs are word for word from the Scriptures, and the tunes are simple and fun. The *G. T.* series even includes the reference in the melody of the song! If you don't have children, Integrity Records has a series of more contemporary adult-oriented songs, all taken directly from the pages of Scripture. Music is a wonderful tool that can help us lock away a passage from the Bible.

Real-Life Impact

Reading, studying, meditating on and memorizing the truth of Scripture are essential parts of our spiritual workout if we hope to grow in godliness. A husband who is spiritually flabby will find himself ill equipped for his role.

That's the lesson Paul Luchsinger learned. In the early 1980s, Paul was a rodeo cowboy with an attitude, on his way to the top of the pro rodeo circuit. At the National Finals in Oklahoma City in 1980, Paul was introduced to Susie McEntire, the pretty redhead who was singing backup for her sister Reba. A year later, Susie and Paul were husband and wife.

It was a matter of weeks before the honeymoon ended, and Susie saw a side of Paul she had never seen during their engagement. In New Mexico one night, Paul and Susie got into an argument that ended with Paul literally throwing his wife out of bed and overturning the mattress so that neither of them could sleep there. Later that night, Paul apologized to his wife, begging for her forgiveness. Susie was terrified. The explosive temper Paul had unleashed that night escalated to ongoing physical and emotional abuse that lasted more than 12 years.

Paul and Susie's secret stayed hidden from family and friends until one day in 1994, when the couple was staying with friends in Billings, Montana. Paul lost his temper with Susie, grabbing her by the neck of her shirt and shoving her against the wall. This time, though, Susie went to the couple with whom they were staying and told them about Paul and his temper. The hidden secret was now out in the open. Their friends helped Paul and Susie get counseling and provided needed accountability.

For Paul, however, the real change came in 1996. He and Susie had taken a sabbatical and had moved to Seattle to be discipled by a pastor there. During that year, Paul and Susie attended a marriage seminar, at which God's Word finally pierced Paul's heart and opened his eyes.

That weekend a series of passages from the Bible brought Paul face-to-face with his anger and his sin. In Isaiah, he read, "All of us like sheep have gone astray, each of us has turned to his own way; but the LORD has caused the iniquity of us all to fall on Him" (53:6). For the first time, Paul saw the selfishness and sin in his own heart. Next, he saw how he

had been trying for years to control his own anger instead of submitting
to the lordship of Christ and allowing Him to transform his life.

Paul also learned how to guard his heart (see Prov. 4:23). He learned
about confession and forgiveness (see 1 John 1:9). He learned how to
walk not in the counsel of the wicked but to delight in the law of the
Lord and meditate in His law day and night (see Ps. 1:1-2). Finally, he
learned how to take every thought—especially the angry ones—captive
(see 2 Cor. 10:5) and to think on that which is pure, lovely, of good
repute, excellent and praiseworthy (see Phil. 4:8).

Those biblical passages had a transforming impact on Paul's life.
Since that time, he has not harmed Susie physically, and he has learned
how to let Christ control his temper. He and Susie still quarrel with each
other, but there is no fear anymore. God's Word has done its transforming work in Paul's life.[4]

In Closing

**God's Word will have the same impact on any man who reads, studies, med-
itates on and memorizes it.** You don't have to change yourself and break
your own bad habits. God's Word is living and powerful. Letting it transform you is the first step toward becoming the kind of man who can love
and lead his wife.

PointstoConsider

1. In the wedding ceremony, you took a vow to remain married "till
   death do us part." What pressures in our culture today make it
   difficult for husbands to remain true to these vows?
2. When have you and your wife drifted toward isolation in your
   marriage? How did it happen?
3. How often do you read the Bible? How often do you read other
   types of printed material? What keeps you from reading the
   Bible more than you do?

4. Read through Psalm 19:7-11. In what ways have you seen the truths in this passage evidenced in your life?

5. How well and how consistently do you *study* the Bible? What opportunities are available to you to study the Word in a group that would provide direction and accountability?

6. Read Psalm 1:1-3. How well does this passage describe you? In what ways have you prospered in the past as you have meditated upon God's Word?

CHAPTER 5

AMANWHO WALKSWITH GOD

Whose job is it to make you into a godly man? Is it your responsibility or God's? That provocative question has confounded and confused Christians throughout the ages. All Christians embrace the biblical truth that a man is saved by the grace of God and not as a result of human effort. But when it comes to our sanctification—our godliness— we're not entirely sure what our part is and what God's part is.

As we've already seen, a godly husband must first be a godly man. He must understand that God made him specially equipped as a man to take initiative, to protect and to provide for himself and for others. He must also be committed to the goal of godliness. Any man can get married. Only a man committed to godliness will have what it takes to fulfill his marriage vows.

How does a man pursue godliness? According to the Bible, it's a matter of training:

> Have nothing to do with godless myths and old wives' tales; rather, *train yourself to be godly*. For physical training is of some value, but godliness has value for all things, holding promise for both the present life and the life to come (1 Tim. 4:7-8, *NIV*, emphasis added).

Grace alone saves you from your sins and makes you right with God. Becoming godly men is also a result of God's grace. The only way your life will be changed is when God changes you. That's the liberating, good news of the gospel. You can grit your teeth and follow the six steps to holy living (whatever they are), only to find yourself ensnared by the enemy of your soul, who wants to render you spiritually impotent.

Paul had to scold the believers in the Galatian Church for their teeth-gritting approach to sanctification. "You foolish Galatians," he wrote, "who has bewitched you, before whose eyes Jesus Christ was publicly portrayed as crucified? This is the only thing I want to find out from you: did you receive the Spirit by the works of the Law, or by hearing with faith? Are you so foolish? Having begun by the Spirit, are you now being perfected by the flesh?" (3:1-3).

Today, many believers find themselves in the same trap. They trusted Christ to redeem them, but they think they are somehow responsible for their own godliness. They began in the Spirit, but they are hoping to be perfected by the flesh. Paul says people who live like that are foolish!

So does a Christian man just sit back? Are we to "let go and let God" as some have suggested? Is there anything we can do to grow in godliness?

According to Paul's letter to Timothy, we can train ourselves to be godly in the same way an athlete trains for his event. We can show up for practice, go through the workouts and apply ourselves to godliness. If we do that, God, by His grace, will transform us into the godly men He wants us to be.

Confused? Does "training yourself for godliness" sound like "perfecting yourself in the flesh"? Does showing up for a spiritual workout sound like gritting your teeth and trying to do better?

Consider this illustration. Let's say you want to be the best basketball player you can be. One day you get a letter in the mail from Michael Jordan, inviting you to drop by his house any time and work out with him. He's heard about your desire, and he wants to do what he can to help you.

Now, you might sit down and jot Michael a note, thanking him for the offer, but telling him you think you can take care of this on your own. If he has any coaching tips he wants to send, or some kind of training video, you'd be happy to look it over, but you don't really have the time to go over to his house every day for your workout.

You might write him a note like that, but I doubt it.

Instead, you would probably relocate your family to Chicago and move as close to his neighborhood as possible. You'd arrive at his house an hour before the workout session was to begin, just so you didn't miss a minute. This would be your chance to learn from the master, and you wouldn't pass up the opportunity for anything!

It would be Michael's job to transform you into the best basketball player you can be. He would get all the credit for changing you. Your job would just be to show up for practice.

If we want to train ourselves for godliness, our job is to show up at the spiritual gym every day. We need to discipline ourselves to go through the workouts, even when we don't want to, and build our spiritual muscles. In the process, God will use our faithfulness to those spiritual workouts to turn us from spiritually flabby men into godly men. Rather than trying to tackle some besetting sin head-on, our job is to keep training ourselves through the use of spiritual disciplines. As we lose the flab, those sins will begin to lose their hold on us.

What kind of workout schedule does a spiritually disciplined man follow? What exercises does he participate in to keep his spiritual muscles from becoming flabby? Just what does it take to lead a spiritually disciplined life?

Pastor and author Don Whitney says God uses three primary catalysts for changing us and conforming us to Christ likeness: (1) He uses other men to sharpen us, as iron sharpens iron (see Prov. 27:17); (2) He uses circumstances to provoke us to obedience (in both of those cases, we are generally the passive recipients of God's working in our lives); and (3) He uses a category of spiritual activities that has classically been referred to as the "Spiritual Disciplines." Whitney writes, "Think of the Spiritual Disciplines as spiritual exercises. To go to your favorite spot for prayer or journaling, for example, is like going to a gym and using a weight machine. As physical disciplines like this promote strength, so the Spiritual Disciplines promote Godliness."[1]

In 1 Timothy 4:7, the apostle tells his protégé to "discipline yourself for the purpose of godliness." The word "discipline" in that passage is the Greek word *gumnasia*, from which we get the word "gymnastics" or "gymnasium." If we hope to live godly lives as believers, we'll need *gumnasia*.

I believe the practice of these spiritual exercises—or disciplines—is a requirement for any man who hopes to be a godly husband. When Paul tells us to work out our salvation with fear and trembling (see Phil. 2:12), he is instructing us to live a spiritually disciplined life in a holy fear of God.

No passage in Scripture provides us with a listing of spiritual disciplines. However, the Scriptures describe activities to which we are clearly called as followers of Christ. A godly man will begin his workout in the Word of God, as we saw in the previous chapter, but he won't quit there.

Prayer

Monica's son was a prodigal. She had tried to raise her boy to follow Christ, but the young man seemed to have no interest in her God or her faith. Just like his father, Monica thought wistfully to herself. The boy was very bright and friendly, but he saw no reason to deny his carnal appetite. By the time he was 18, he had fathered an illegitimate son, with no apparent sense of shame or responsibility.

The boy readily acknowledged the existence of God, but he preferred a view of God that allowed him to indulge his passions without fear of repercussions. He talked easily and willingly about religion, and he drifted in and out of various religious philosophies. Now in his early 20s, he had moved away from home and was training to be a teacher.

Except for an occasional letter, Monica rarely heard from her son. She cringed to think of the lifestyle he might be living. Since her husband did not share her faith in Christ or her views on morality, Monica was left alone in her anxiety and grief for her only child.

Her friends at church were empathetic and asked from time to time what news she had heard from her son. Monica would tell them about the latest letter she had received, which was often months old. In spite of their compassion for her, she felt helpless and alone.

Every day she prayed. She poured out her heart to God, begging Him to protect her son from evil. She prayed for godly men to come into his life, men who might somehow be able to penetrate his skepticism and his selfishness. Months turned into years as this faithful mother daily petitioned God to bring home her wayward son.

When he was 30, the young man moved to a new city in search of a better teaching position. There, unbeknown to his mother, he struck up a friendship with a local pastor who was every bit his match in intellect and rhetorical skills. The two visited often, and the pastor was eventually able to persuade the young teacher that his objections to Christianity were based mostly on misconceptions of the faith. He still had many questions, though. If God really is sovereign and supreme, how could evil exist? He remained a skeptic, in spite of his growing understanding of biblical Christianity.

One summer afternoon, when he was 32, the young man was sitting in a courtyard, thinking through his life and his bumpy journey from one spiritual philosophy to the next, when he heard the voice of a child from beyond the fence. The voice interrupted his contemplation, and the words, "take up and read," caught his attention. Somehow the young teacher knew those words were meant for him. He went and found a copy of the New Testament, which had been given to him by a friend. He opened the book randomly, and his eyes fell on this passage:

Let us behave properly as in the day, not in carousing and drunkenness, not in sexual promiscuity and sensuality, not in strife and jealousy. But put on the Lord Jesus Christ, and make no provision for the flesh in regard to its lusts (Rom. 13:13-14).

The young teacher would later write in his autobiography, "I had no wish to read further and no need to do so. For in an instant, as I came to the end of the sentence, it was as though the light of faith flooded into my heart and all the darkness of doubt was dispelled."[2]

When eventually the good news of her son's conversion reached her, Monica rejoiced as she wept. Not only had her prayers for her son been answered, but God had also used her faithful and reverent spirit to bring her husband to a saving knowledge of Christ. Monica died at 56, in peace, praising God for His gracious answer to her prayers. What she didn't know in this life was that her son would eventually give his life to serve the Church and would become perhaps the most influential churchman in history. This young teacher, Augustine, through his writing and his teaching, continues to shed light on our understanding of the Bible and what it means to be a follower of Christ.

Effects of Prayer

Would Augustine have been converted without the prayers of his mother? One of the mysteries of our relationship with God is how our prayers affect His sovereign purposes. C. S. Lewis wrestled with this question in an essay written in 1945 entitled "Work or Prayer." In it, he states the case against prayer, which is that God doesn't need the ill-informed and contradictory advice of humans on how to run the world. He already knows what is best, and being benevolent, He will do what needs to be done whether we pray or not.

With his usual insight, Lewis points out that such a view would leave us wondering why Jesus taught us to pray in Matthew 6. The Lord Himself instructed His followers to pray for daily bread and for protection from temptation and evil. He goes on to point out that the argument against prayer—God knows best and is going to do whatever He pleases anyway—is ultimately an argument against everything. "Why wash your hands?" he asks. "If God intends them to be clean, they'll come clean without your washing them. If He doesn't, they'll remain dirty (as Lady Macbeth found) however much soap you use. Why ask for the salt? Why put on your boots? Why do anything?"[3]

The spiritual discipline of prayer has become obscured in our day because we have allowed our own selfishness to dominate our understanding of what prayer means. We have become like college students who call home only when their checking account is low. We are quick to cry out to God when we face difficult circumstances beyond our control, and just as quick to ignore the discipline of prayer when everything is going smoothly. Prayer has become synonymous with "asking God for something." Any other reason for prayer has become superfluous.

Purpose of Prayer

If we are to participate meaningfully in the discipline of prayer, we need to understand its purposes beyond making petitions of the King. We need to see it in its biblical light before we'll understand how God uses this activity to make us more like Christ.

In 1 Thessalonians 5:17, Paul exhorts us with a startling three-word declaration: "Pray without ceasing." Now, if we're limited by a head-bowed, eyes-closed understanding of prayer, we will wind up leading a rather limited existence. That verse is a challenge to walk every minute of our lives in constant communion with Christ. To "pray without ceasing" means, in the words of Brother Andrew, to "practice the presence of God."

Think for a minute about the dark-suited, sunglasses-wearing secret service men you've seen protecting the President or other government officials. In addition to whatever gun they may be carrying, each of them is equipped with the requisite earpiece—a device that looks like a hearing aid with a cord that disappears into a pocket somewhere. At the other end of that listening device is someone who is running the security detail, probably someone who has a better vantage point and can alert the agents to people or things they might not be able to see themselves. That earpiece goes everywhere with the agent, and whenever he is on duty, the listening device is on.

Couple that earpiece with a transmitter for two-way communication, and you have a picture of how a Christian is supposed to stay in contact with God. A follower of Christ is always alert, listening, mindful of his assignment and—to borrow again from law enforcement—always "on the radio."

Instructions on Prayer

In addition to being in constant communion with God, we are to spend regular periods of time in focused, one-on-one interaction with our creator. What a privilege! To have access to the throne room of heaven any time we choose is a divine benefit we should not ignore.

Our instructions from Jesus on how to pray (see Matt. 6:9-13) offer us a pattern for prayer that will move us from a litany of selfish requests to a better understanding of God's purposes. John MacArthur, in his book *Jesus' Pattern for Prayer*, points out that what we commonly know as the Lord's Prayer was never intended to be recited merely as a part of a liturgical ritual, but instead was meant to be a guide for prayer.

According to Jesus, we are to begin our prayers by honoring our Father. For Jews who refused to even speak the name of God, it was a radical paradigm shift for them to address their prayers to a heavenly "Father." By addressing God as Father, we acknowledge that our access to His throne room is predicated on our having been adopted into His family. We can call Him Abba only if His Spirit has first converted us.

In directing us to hallow God's name, we are invited to rehearse His majestic attributes. Think of all the ways God is distinct from His creation. He is omniscient; we have finite knowledge and understanding. He is all-powerful; we are weak. He is perfectly righteous; we are stained with sin. As we consider His unique characteristics, we become aware of the significance of our communion with Him.

Jesus then instructs us to recommit ourselves in prayer to obeying His commandments. Christians today have made "recommitment" into a new sacrament, where we go forward at the end of a worship service to rededicate ourselves as believers. When we pray, "Your will be done," we are daily recommitting ourselves to a life of service and sacrifice for the cause of Christ.

Our petitions follow our pledge to do His will. When we ask God for anything, it is always with the understanding that we want first and foremost those things that will advance His Kingdom and will honor His name. Any request we make is done in that context, acknowledging Him as the all-wise and all-loving ruler of the universe, whose ways are far beyond our understanding.

We are instructed to confess our sins to God, and not because He doesn't already know what we've done. He not only knows, but He also has paid the penalty for those sins. In seeking forgiveness for sins, we are asking God, as David did in Psalm 51, to restore to us the joy of our salvation and to renew a right spirit in us. Our forgiveness was accomplished at the Cross. Our prayer of confession reminds us of our utter dependence on the grace of God for the gracious gift of eternal life.

We also pray to God for guidance and wisdom, "do not lead us into temptation, but deliver us from evil" (Matt. 6:13), acknowledging again our need for the ministry of the Holy Spirit to direct our lives. Our hearts are deceitful, the prophet Jeremiah says (see 17:9). In Proverbs, we learn that the way that seems right to us ends in death (see 16:25). In asking God to lead us, we again subject our will and our desires to the higher calling of His Kingdom and His glory.

Think for a minute about the last time you were in a group where someone asked for prayer requests. Without having been there, I can probably guess that the majority of the requests were for someone who was sick (and it was probably someone other than the person making the request). I have wondered on occasion if one of the reasons God doesn't redeem our bodies at the same time that he redeems our souls is because He wants us to have something that will remind us of our dependence on Him, driving us back to Him in prayer.

God does not instruct us to pray because He needs our advice. He doesn't ask us to pray so that we might tell Him something He doesn't already know. His invitation for us to spend time in communion and in conversation with Him is not, as some have suggested, because He longs to spend time with us. He instructs us to pray so that our hearts, our minds and our actions might be yielded to His perfect will. In prayer, God takes a man who, as the old hymn says, has a heart that is prone to wander, and He guides him in paths of righteousness for His own name's sake.

When a man disciplines himself to pray regularly, he will grow in masculine godliness.

Worship

In the same way that prayer focuses our mind in communicating to God, worship—a focused expression of praise and adoration to Christ—tunes our hearts to sing his grace.[4] "An hour is coming," Jesus said, "and now is, when the true worshipers will worship the Father in spirit and truth; for such people the Father seeks to be His worshipers" (John 4:23).

Worship incorporates the disciplines we've already examined. To worship the Father in truth requires reading, study, meditation and memorization of God's Word. To worship Him in Spirit means that our inner self—the nonmaterial part of man—communes with God, who is Spirit. Worship is the total response of our life to the life of Christ. That's why Paul charges us to present our bodies as "a living and holy sacrifice, acceptable to God, which is your spiritual service of worship" (Rom. 12:1). Worship involves our mind, our emotions, our bodies—our entire being—responding to the incredible worth of God.

In fact, that's where the English word "worship" comes from. The original Anglo-Saxon word was *worthship*. David understood the idea of worship when he wrote:

> Ascribe to the LORD, O sons of the mighty, ascribe to the LORD glory and strength. Ascribe to the LORD the glory due to His name; worship the LORD in holy array (Ps. 29:1-2).

Love the Lord

Several years ago, our family relocated from one city to another. I had already made the transition to the new city to begin working while Mary Ann prepared our belongings to be moved and showed our home to prospective buyers. On Sundays, I visited some of the churches in the area to consider where our family would attend once the move was complete.

I arrived at one church just as the morning service was beginning. The words to the hymns were being projected on a screen in the front of the auditorium, and the music director was seated at his piano on the platform. I sat a few rows from the back, alone, to "check this new church out."

Now, I tend to be a pretty stoic individual. I keep my emotions under control. When people around me lose their composure, I can typically maintain mine. (The most notable exception to that rule is when the telegram arrives from Sam Wainwright in the final scene of *It's a Wonderful Life*—I have to wipe away tears every year, even though I've seen the same scene two dozen times!)

I don't know all the factors that morning in church, but I found myself with tears in my eyes in the middle of singing hymns to God. In that moment, I was weeping for joy as I expressed my thanks and praise to God for His grace and mercy in my life.

Tears are not the hallmark of genuine worship, by any means. But when Jesus was asked to sum up all that is required of us in the Law, He replied by charging that we are to love the Lord our God with our heart, our mind, our soul and our strength (see Matt. 22:37). Worship is all that we are, expressing praise and thanksgiving to God for all that He is.

Worship in Spirit and in Truth

In the Scriptures, we see that worship is done publicly and privately. It is both a corporate discipline for the Church and a private response to God by an individual. It is expressed in words, in actions and in the quiet meditation of our hearts.

One of the great gifts God has given us, as a tool for worshiping Him, is music. Paul explains that as the Word of Christ dwells in us, we will respond by "teaching and admonishing one another with psalms and hymns and spiritual songs, singing with thankfulness in your hearts to God" (Col. 3:16). When we are filled with the Spirit, He says, we will speak "to one another in psalms and hymns and spiritual songs, singing and making melody with your heart to the Lord" (Eph. 5:19).

In the office building where I work, there is a flight of stairs that leads from my office on the third floor to the lobby. The stairwell is one of the most perfect reverb chambers I've ever heard, as sound echoes off the walls.

Some nights, when I'm leaving the office late, I'll walk into the stairwell and begin to sing as I descend the stairs. The acoustics of that area can make even a melodically challenged baritone sound like he's ready for the recording studio! Somehow, as the sound of "Holy, Holy, Holy" or "Crown Him with Many Crowns" reverberates in that stairwell, I find my heart swelling up in praise of God. It is one of my favorite places for private worship!

Often you'll hear people use the term "worship" interchangeably with congregational singing. "The worship was wonderful this morning," they'll say, when what they mean was they liked the songs. Music may serve as a call to worship or as a response to the preaching of God's Word, but worship involves more than just singing. As we listen to God's Word being preached, read the Bible together in a service, pray or recite a creed—all of that is worship. Music is just one powerful element that connects with our heart and mind and ought to draw us into an attitude of reverence for God.

I'm concerned that much of what passes for worship today is more trivial than transcendent. Many of the new songs we sing tend to focus more on God's provision for our needs than they do on His holy attributes and His character. The songs are loaded down with "I," "me" and "my," and offer only a token reference to God being there or Jesus caring about our hurts and our pain. They tend to express love for God in almost romantic terms.

As the Psalms—the hymnbook of the nation of Israel—shows, there is a place for praise and thankfulness being expressed to God in response to His providence and His grace. We are told to bless the Lord and to forget none of His benefits. We read David praise God for answering him when he cried out, "I will sing to the LORD, because He has dealt bountifully with me" (13:6).

But the major theme of our worship should be the theme of Scripture—the glory of God made manifest to us in His redemption of His Church. As one contemporary chorus suggests, "Let's forget about ourselves and magnify the Lord and worship Him." Good advice. Many of the great hymns of the faith combine majestic melodies with lyrics that are profound and theologically accurate.

In his book *Sacred Pathways*, Gary Thomas finds nine "pathways to God" in the pages of Scripture. These pathways are different ways in which people tend to be drawn into a spirit of worship. Some people find themselves more ready to worship in an outdoor setting than in a church building. For others, majestic architecture and stained glass inspire a heart of worship. Still, another can walk out of a lecture in a seminary classroom with a heart full of praise or reverence for God, while a different individual finds that acts of charity or service inspires her to worship.

No single pathway is the biblically approved path to God, Thomas argues. Paul, Peter and David might all have worshiped God with very different styles. The point is that they all worshiped in spirit and in truth. Those are the worshipers God is seeking to worship Him.

For you, worship may involve singing along to a CD on the way to or from work. You may use the *Book of Common Prayer* for a daily time of prayer and worship. Whatever pathway you choose, you need to be preparing yourself for the day when you will join with tens of thousands of worshipers, gathered around the throne of God, singing, "Worthy is the Lamb that was slain to receive power and riches and wisdom and might and honor and glory and blessing" (Rev. 5:12).

When a man disciplines himself to reverently worship God, he will grow in masculine godliness.

Community

When Adam stood by himself in the garden, God said, "It is not good for the man to be alone" (Gen. 2:18).

When the creator had joined the first couple together in marriage, He pronounced His mandate: "Be fruitful and multiply" (1:22).

And as Abraham stood on a Judean hillside, staring at the sky, he heard the voice of God speak to him, saying, "I will make you a great nation, and I will bless you, and make your name great; and so you shall be a blessing" (12:2).

First, marriage; then, family. Finally, a nation of men and women who trust in Yahweh.

God's plan for man is built around relationships. He made us social beings who need each other as much as we need Him.

Read that last sentence again. It almost sounds like heresy in a culture that honors rugged individualism. Undoubtedly, somewhere along the line, you've heard (or maybe even said yourself), "God is all I need."

But the God who created you made you with a need for relationships with other people. His plan has always been to meet some of your needs through His servants. Remember, Adam walked with God in the cool of the day in paradise, just the way God had created him, when the creator made the startling statement, "It is *not* good" (2:18, emphasis added).

That same God, incarnate in Jesus Christ, gathered around Him 12 followers. When He sent them out into the surrounding villages and towns to proclaim that the kingdom of God had come, He sent them out in pairs (see Luke 10:1). After His resurrection, His followers were commissioned to make disciples, and they obeyed their master not by simply preaching the gospel but by establishing churches throughout the Roman Empire. They understood that disciple-making required community.

Understanding the Purposes of Community

In Scripture, God has established three social institutions to carry out His plan for men. The first is the family. It's the priority. It is the primary social institution in every culture. As you will learn in this book, a husband bears the weight of leadership at home.

God has also ordained that the government is to be established under His Lordship, to carry out His purposes in a society. Kings rule on Earth, but only at God's behest. He works through governing authorities to carry out His will, whether for blessing or for judgment. "The king's heart is like channels of water in the hand of the LORD; He turns it wherever He wishes" (Prov. 21:1).

The final institution ordained by God is His own Body, the Church, made up of men and women who name Jesus Christ as Lord and who gather for the preaching of the Word and the administration of the sacraments. That community of people, God has said, need not fear the gates of hell (see Matt. 16:18). He has established His Church.

Over the last 30 or 40 years, we have seen what sociologist Robert Bellah calls our culture of "radical individualism" pollute and distort what we understand about the Church. By inviting men and women to have a "personal relationship with Christ," and by stressing how we can know God personally, we have obscured the bigger picture. "There is no such thing," says Chuck Colson, "as Christianity apart from the church."[5] Saint Augustine made a similar statement that sounds almost unorthodox to our "personal relationship with God" culture. He said, "He cannot have God for his Father who does not have the church for his mother." Luther stated it even stronger: "Apart from the church, salvation is impossible."[6] And John Calvin emphasized the same point this way: "So highly does the Lord esteem the communion of his church that he considers everyone a traitor and apostate from religion who perversely withdraws himself from any Christian society which preserves the true ministry of the word and sacraments."[7]

Those who have looked to the pages of Scripture to find the purpose for the Church have routinely cited two passages. In Acts 2:42, we read that the first-century believers "were continually devoting themselves to the apostles' teaching and to fellowship, to the breaking of bread and to prayer." Those four activities get to the core of what the Church is supposed to be doing. Paul says that God has gifted certain men within the church "for the equipping of the saints for the work of service, to the building up of the body of Christ; until we all attain to the unity of the faith, and of the knowledge of the Son of God, to a mature man, to the measure of the stature which belongs to the fullness of Christ" (Eph. 4:12-13).

The apostle Paul also stresses our interdependence in the Body of Christ in his first letter to the Corinthian Church. Using the analogy of the human body and its interdependent members, he writes:

> But now God has placed the members, each one of them, in the body, just as He desired. And if they were all one member, where would the body be? But now there are many members, but one body. And the eye cannot say to the hand, "I have no need of you"; or again the head to the feet, "I have no need of you" (1 Cor. 12:18-21).

His point is obvious. There are no "lone rangers" in the Body of Christ.

Throughout the New Testament, we are constantly reminded that God's plan for us requires community. We are told to love one another, to serve one another, and to be devoted to and give preference to one another. We would have to examine more than 50 passages in the Epistles alone to understand our responsibilities to "one another" within the community of faith.

Preparing Through Participation in Community

When we talk about the discipline of community, we are talking about active participation in the life of the Church. Not membership. Not attendance. Not singing in the choir or teaching Sunday School to four-year-olds. As valuable as those things are, the heart of what God wants for His Church is what the Apostles' Creed calls "the communion of the saints."

In the process of learning, worshiping, praying and breaking bread with other believers, God intends to press us toward maturity in Christ. Part of His brilliant design involves gifting us all differently so we will press beyond our natural individualistic instincts toward one another. In the process, God says, iron can sharpen iron (see Prov. 27:17).

When a man disciplines himself to active participation in a community of faith, he will grow in masculine godliness.

In Closing

We have by no means exhausted the list of spiritual exercises or disciplines that we can use to train ourselves for godliness. In fasting, for example, we learn the discipline of self-denial. In solitude, we learn to slow down to listen to the voice of the Spirit. In service, we learn to focus on others as more important than ourselves. Other disciplines, such as stewardship and simplicity, are used by God to conform us to the image of Christ.

These disciplines need to be resident in your own soul, not only for your spiritual growth, but also because (as we'll see later) you bear the responsibility as a husband for making these disciplines a part of your marriage and family. You should be the one prompting your wife to read and study her Bible. You are to encourage her to meditate on and memorize passages of Scripture, to pray, to worship Christ and to be an active part of a community of faith.

A godly man, then, is a man who knows what it means to fear the Lord, and who disciplines himself for godliness. Only at this point is he ready to assume the responsibilities that come with being a husband.

PointstoConsider

1. What do you think it means to be a "godly" man?
2. Read Galatians 3:1-3. In what ways have you fallen into the trap of assuming responsibility for your own godliness?
3. Read 1 Timothy 4:7-8. What does it mean to "discipline yourself for the purpose of godliness"?
4. How would you rate yourself in the following spiritual disciplines?

   · Prayer
   · Worship
   · Community

5. What does it mean to "pray without ceasing," as Paul exhorts us in 1 Thessalonians 5:17? How can you do this, in practical terms?
6. What does it mean to worship God "in spirit and truth," as Jesus says in John 4:23?
7. In what ways are you tempted toward radical individualism—the belief that you need nobody else?
8. What does 1 Corinthians 12:18-21 say about our need for other Christians? In what ways have you seen these truths become evident in your own life?

PART TWO

THE
MODELFOR
HUSBANDS:
JESUSCHRIST

"Welcome back, Mr. Lepine."

"Thanks."

"I have reviewed the results of your initial screening exam and you meet the minimum qualifications as a candidate for the position."

"That test was pretty hard. I didn't know if I was gonna pass or not!"

"Your test scores show that you have a satisfactory understanding of your own masculinity and that you know the characteristics of a godly man. On the application section, you demonstrated a minimum level of proficiency, but there is much room for growth."

"Yeah, I felt like I was doing okay till I got to that part of the test. Frankly, I thought I had probably flunked the part on discipline and the stuff about godly character."

"The instrument we use is designed to measure progress, not proficiency. We are more interested to see that a candidate is growing and moving in the right direction. We have more success with those candidates than we do with the ones who exhibit a level of competency but who don't seem to be making progress."

"So what now?"

"You have cleared the first hurdle. All candidates who meet the minimum qualifications are invited to take a second exam."

"You know, I never have tested well."

"This exam will measure your understanding of the office to which you aspire. We want to see how much you know about the role a husband is called to play."

"The 'love your wife' stuff we talked about last time?"

"Not yet. Before we look at how much you know about how a husband functions day to day, we want to measure your understanding of the responsibilities you will assume in the position."

"I've been reading that part in Ephesians 5 that you talked about last time."

"That's fine, Mr. Lepine. Here, though, we want to focus on
1 Corinthians 11."

"Uh-oh. I didn't know I was supposed to know that part."

"Most candidates don't. Let me read it to you. It's just one verse,
verse 3. It says, 'But I want you to understand that Christ is
the head of every man, and the man is the head of a woman,
and God is the head of Christ.'"

"You mean 'head' as in 'head'? Like a boss?"

"In one sense. The idea of headship really means . . . "

"Do you know if Mary Ann knows about this verse? I don't think
she agrees with it."

"A lot of people misunderstand . . . "

"I mean, we've talked about it, and we think marriage ought to
be more like a partnership, you know? Not a dictatorship,
with me bossing everyone around."

"That is not what we mean by 'head,' Mr. Lepine. We're not looking for dictators here."

"Well, it sure sounds that way."

"Look back at the verse with me. Is Christ the 'dictator' for every
man? Is God the 'boss' of Christ?"

"No."

"So that would rule out the boss or dictator approach to headship, wouldn't it?"

"Yeah. I thought God and Christ are supposed to be equal—the
same."

"Equal, yes. The same, no. The Father and the Son have equal
value and essence but have different functions. God the
Father functions as the head of God the Son. God the Son
obeys and submits to God the Father."

"So you're saying that a husband and wife have equal value, but
that a husband is the head and the wife has to obey him?"

"Mr. Lepine, there is a lot of confusion and misunderstanding
about this whole idea. Let me make a suggestion. We offer
a training course called, 'The General Responsibilities of a
Husband.' It examines the office of husband and explains

how he is to be a prophet, a priest and a king for his wife and
his family."

"I thought priests weren't supposed to get married."

"Ahh . . . I'm going to recommend you take the course before
you take the second exam. I think it may clear up some of
your confusion."

"I'm not sure what Mary Ann is going to think about this headship thing. Being a spiritual leader is one thing, but being
the head is something else."

"The truth is, Mr. Lepine, many wives struggle with the concept
of male headship. It goes all the way back to Eve. Do you
want to become the kind of husband Mary Ann wants you to
be? Or do you want to become the kind of husband God
wants you to be?"

"But if she doesn't go for it . . . "

"We'll leave that part up to God. He has some experience with
this issue."

"Okay. I guess if I want the job, I'd better learn how to do it
right."

Leading Versus Lording

**Just what does the Bible mean when it teaches in 1 Corinthians 11 that
the man is the head of the woman?** That issue has been the subject of
great misunderstanding and heated debate over the last half century.
In his excellent study of male and female roles in marriage entitled
Rockin' the Roles, Dr. Robert Lewis suggests that many men have abused
the concept of headship and assumed the role of despot in their home.
They have become what he calls "lording leaders" who fail to reflect
Christlike humility and service in their relationships. Their model for
headship seems to have been the Pharaohs of Egypt more than the
Lamb of God.

Women have rightly rebelled against this kind of dictatorship in
marriage, but many have thrown out the proverbial baby with the bath
water. Some have suggested that the word "head" in the Scriptures was

not intended to ordain some position of leadership in a marriage. Instead, they say, the word "head" means "source," in the same way that the headwaters of a river are the source of the stream. They go from that premise to begin a series of theological back flips and cartwheels, trying to explain that "head" simply means that Adam was the source of Eve, and that a man today is to be the source of nourishment for his wife.[1]

The objections to the traditional understanding of headship are directed more at the abuses of the biblical idea than they are rooted in New Testament scholarship. The idea that God would ordain any hierarchical structure to male/female relationships is repugnant to the critics, seeming to imply a limited role and a limited value to women in the home and in the Church. In the same way, the concept of female submission seems demeaning and degrading to the worth of a woman.

Certainly, biblical passages have been misunderstood and misapplied by some in a way that has devalued a woman's role in the home and in the Church. But those abuses do not constitute grounds for attempting to reinvent a meaning for difficult biblical passages. Our goal should be to better understand the way in which Christ serves as the head of His Church or in which God is the head of Christ, in order to know how a man should be the head of a woman.

Before the coming of Christ, God led the nation of Israel through a variety of human agents. Originally, the nation looked to its patriarchs for divine guidance. Abraham, Isaac and Jacob were the fathers who heard from God and who led their families. As the families grew into tribes, patriarchal leadership became impossible. With the wise counsel of his father-in-law, Jethro, Moses appointed judges to settle disputes among the people.

Ultimately, the leadership of the nation rested in three places. First, God raised up prophets who continued the patriarchal role of hearing from God and speaking on His behalf to His people. Second, God appointed a line of priests to attend to the spiritual needs of His people and to serve as the mediators between God and man by offering the sacrifice for sin. Finally, somewhat reluctantly, God allowed for the nation to be led by a king who was charged with responsibility for the physical needs of the nation.

John Calvin taught that the office which Christ "received from the Father consists of three parts. For he was appointed . . . Prophet, King and Priest."[2] Christ's headship, according to Calvin, involves the perfect fulfillment of the Old Testament types. Christ is, according to the author of Hebrews, our High Priest and eternal King, after the order of Melchizedek (see 6:20; 7:1-2), and God's prophet during the last days (see 1:1-2). Further, the messianic title of Christ—"anointed one"—refers to the anointing with holy oil that was, under the law, given to prophets, priests and kings.

Today, Christ is the head of His Church by serving as prophet, priest and King. If a man is to be the head of the woman in the same way Christ is the head of the Church, then as husbands, we must understand the prophetic, priestly and kingly roles we are to fulfill. The subsequent chapters show how a husband can follow the example of Christ in leading his wife.

CHAPTER 6

THE HUSBAND WHO LEADS IN PRAYER

After more than a year of living on the ark with all the animals, what was the first thing Noah did when he and his family stepped onto dry ground? Hold that thought.

Hard times had fallen on the settlements in colonial New England in 1679. Almost 100 years before the Revolutionary War, the General Court of the Massachusetts Colony wondered aloud if the disease, the crop failures and the other hardships they were experiencing were a result of divine judgment. This was a time, unlike the present, when men were wise enough to see both the hand of providence and the hand of judgment present in the affairs of men.

The Synod of New England, made up of pastors and elders from churches throughout the area, met to determine a course of action.

Together, they prayed, debated and considered why the hand of God seemed to be chastening His people. In the end, they listed 14 reasons for what they viewed as divine judgment.

One of the reasons they highlighted was the breakdown in the practice of family worship. "There are many families," the Synod wrote, "that do not pray to God constantly, morning and evening, and many more where the Scriptures are not daily read so that the Word of Christ might richly dwell in them. There are too many houses that are full of ignorance and profaneness and that are not duly examined and for this cause wrath may come upon others around themselves (see Joshua 22:20; Jeremiah 5:7; 10:25). Many householders who profess religion do not cause all that are within their gates to become subject unto good order as they ought (see Exodus 20:10). . . . Most of the evils that abound among us proceed from defects in family government."[1]

Imagine what the Synod of New England would say about the spiritual condition of families today! We struggle as families to squeeze in a devotional activity from time to time, and we feel compelled to make the activity fun and engaging so our children will like it. Three hundred years ago, a Christian husband was more interested in bringing his family into the presence of God than whether or not the children were enjoying themselves in the process.

A husband is, by God's design, the priest of his family. Long before the Levites were set apart as the priestly line, and the sons of Aaron were established as the priests of the nation, the patriarchs assumed a priestly role, interceding for their families (as Abraham did when God announced His judgment of Sodom) and offering sacrifices to Yahweh.

Which brings us back to Noah. After seeing the wrath of God poured out on all men because of their wickedness and their failure to worship Him, Noah called his sons together as soon as the ark was on dry land, and he offered a sacrifice to God. Undoubtedly, he wanted to give thanks to God for sparing his family. But he also must have been acutely aware of his own sins and the sins of his family, especially after living in close quarters with a boatload of wild animals for more than a year. With the judgment of God fresh on his mind, Noah sought atonement by offering sacrifices:

Then Noah built an altar to the LORD, and took of every clean animal and of every clean bird and offered burnt offerings on the altar. The LORD smelled the soothing aroma; and the LORD said to Himself, "I will never again curse the ground on account of man, for the intent of man's heart is evil from his youth; and I will never again destroy every living thing, as I have done" (Gen. 8:20-21).

The role of the priest, according to the Scriptures, is to hear from God's people and lead them before His throne. He intercedes for them, speaking to God on their behalf. He is not, as some have suggested, the intermediary between God and man. The Bible makes it clear that "there is one God, and one mediator also between God and men, the man Christ Jesus" (1 Tim. 2:5). The Bible also affirms that each believer is invited directly into the presence of God on the basis of Christ's sacrifice. Peter tells us that as the people of God we are, among other things, "a royal priesthood" (1 Pet. 2:9).

Still, husbands are responsible to serve a priestly function in their homes. We have the holy duty of leading our wives and our families into God's presence for worship, reminding them of God's grace and mercy in the forgiveness of their sins and offering intercession on their behalf.

The Worship-Leading Husband

In the glove compartment of our eight-year-old minivan is a hymnal. My wife placed it there as a sleep aid for our children. Let me explain.

When our first child was a baby, we often found ourselves on long trips with a fussy infant or toddler, perched in her car seat, refusing to nap and wanting to be taken out and held. It's one thing to let your child cry herself to sleep when she's in her crib and you can shut the door to her room, but when she's three feet away from you and trying desperately to stay awake, it's a challenge just to maintain your sanity!

During one of those early trips, I launched into an a cappella version of "It Is Well with My Soul." The sound of singing startled our daughter enough to stop her crying momentarily. Mary Ann joined in on the second line. The baby started whimpering again and eventually was back to full volume. As she got louder, so did we, moving on to "Crown Him with Many Crowns" and "All Hail the Power of Jesus' Name." After 10 or 15 minutes, she was giving up and nodding off to sleep. Meanwhile, we had found ourselves enjoying our two-person choir, with Mary Ann finding the alto line to add to my melody.

Admittedly, we did not have a particularly spiritual motive for our traveling chorus of hymns. Our purpose was utilitarian, not transcendent. But as we tried to remember the second and third verses of hymns (the reason a hymnal was later added to the vehicle), we found ourselves reminded of the One about whom we were singing: immortal, invisible, holy creator of the rolling spheres, ineffably sublime! Even after our child was sleeping, we continued to sing psalms, hymns and spiritual songs, making melody in our hearts and on our lips (see Eph. 5:19).

When God established the Levitical priesthood in ancient Israel, He charged them to lead the nation in the corporate worship of God. The priests maintained the Temple. They were to make sure the eternal flame on the altar burned day and night (see Lev. 6:12; 2 Chron. 13:11). They kept the golden lampstands filled with oil so that there was always light in the Temple (see Exod. 27:20-21; Lev. 24:2). They alone were given the assignment of offering sacrifices to God. In fact, when King Saul and King Uzziah assumed the priestly mantle and offered a sacrifice, God judged them for their sin.

In the same way that the Levitical priests superintended the worship of the Israelites, a husband should function as the worship leader for his marriage. He should set apart his home as a temple of God, keeping it holy and undefiled. The flame of God's Spirit should burn brightly in his own heart and in his home. He is to guard the Word of God in his home, making sure it is honored by all. And he should be the one who reminds his wife and his family of the once-for-all sacrifice of Christ made on our behalf.

Lead Daily Worship

As we've already seen, worship involves a lot more than just singing hymns and praise songs. When we talk about a husband as a worship leader, we're talking about more than singing. First, with his wife, and later, as God provides him with children, a husband should assume the responsibility of leading his family into the presence of God. He should initiate prayer with his wife, not only at meals, but at different times during the day. He should make regular church attendance a family priority. He should read the Scriptures with his wife and his children. He should lead the family in songs of praise to God.

In his booklet *Rediscovering the Lost Treasure of Family Worship*, Pastor Jerry Marcellino suggests that husbands lead their wives and their children in a daily worship time that might begin with singing, leading to a time of reading or studying God's Word and concluding with prayer.[2] The whole event may only last for 10 minutes (or might go as long as 30 minutes) and could occur at the end of a meal. A hymn or two (even a tone-deaf husband can invite his wife to join him as they sing along with a CD), a passage from the Bible and a time for family prayer is a daily habit that ought to begin on the first morning of the honeymoon!

As the years go by, the husband-priest in a family can fulfill his duties by not only reminding his family of God's faithfulness seen in the pages of Scripture, but he also can bring to mind their own experience of God's faithfulness. Often, as the people gathered to give thanks to God or to offer a sacrifice, the priest would begin by reciting the history of the nation of Israel, so that each generation might know the wonderful works of God done in their midst. A husband can recall for his family the way in which they have seen God work to provide and protect their family.

A part of the priestly responsibilities in worship is the task of regularly reminding his wife and family of God's grace and mercy in forgiving sins. He declares God's love for them, reminding them that their heavenly Father has cast their sins into the depths of the sea (see Mic. 7:19). He has hidden them behind His back (see Isa. 38:17). He has chosen to remember them no more (see Heb. 8:12).

The central theme of the Bible, crying out from every page, is the proclamation that sins are forgiven in Christ. If our worship is to be complete, whether in church or at home, it should include the declaration of the gospel. That doesn't mean a husband is regularly inviting his wife or his children to pray the sinner's prayer. The gospel is not simply an evangelistic appeal. Instead, it is a regular reminder to God's people that we have been redeemed by His grace. Our goodness can't save us, because we can never be good enough to earn our place in heaven. Our hearts deceive us, the Scriptures teach (see Jer. 17:9), and we need to be reminded of the truth that Christ, who is faithful and just, has cleansed us from all unrighteousness (see 1 John 1:9).

Resume Leadership Responsibilities

Too many husbands assume their spiritual leadership in this area will begin once the children are older. In truth, it begins the day the spiritual responsibility for a young woman is passed from father to husband. In our contemporary, individualistic, egalitarian culture, many husbands reject their priestly responsibilities with their wives (I was one of them), thinking, *She's fully capable of having her own quiet time or doing her own Bible reading.* Besides, we think, we'll just embarrass ourselves. The mature, godly man will not shy away. He will assume his role as priest for his wife and understand it is a necessary function of being called her husband.

In recalling the story of Daniel, the Puritan pastor Samuel Davies reminds us:

> Daniel ran the risk of his life rather than omit this duty of daily worship of God, which some of us omit with hardly any temptation. When the royal edict prohibited him upon penalty of being cast into the lions' den, "he still prayed and gave thanks to God, as he did aforetime."[3]

Today, we need a courageous generation of Daniel-like husbands to resume their responsibilities as a worship leader for their wives and families.

The Intercessor Husband

It was shaping up to be the most stressful night of his life. After years of consistent hard work and growing prominence, he knew everything was about to change—fast. For weeks now, powerful, highly placed men had been mapping out a plan designed to put an end to his growing influence in the community. He—and his work—scared them, and he knew it. They had trumped up charges against him that were scurrilous, but his opponents were powerful men who could make even false charges stick—they had the political clout to buy themselves a few favors.

He had spent the evening having dinner with a group of his coworkers, his closest friends. Although he knew what the next 24 hours would bring, his friends were clueless. It wasn't that they hadn't heard the talk on the street. They simply assumed their boss would once again get himself out of whatever jam he might be in. He knew better. *Not this time*, he thought. *This time there is no Elijah-like disappearance—no last-minute heroics.*

As they talked over dinner, he had tried to prepare them for what was about to happen. There was a lot of silence, blank stares, a few questions. For the most part, though, his friends weren't sure—or they didn't want to believe—what he was telling them. No matter what happened, he told them, they shouldn't worry. He had to go away for a while, but he'd be back for them. In the meantime, they needed to brace themselves, he warned. Everything was about to unravel.

Now, with dinner over, he asked his friends to spend a few minutes praying with him. The emotional stress of all he was facing was overwhelming, and he needed these men to lock arms with him as they prayed for all that was about to happen.

He bowed his head and began to speak to God as easily and comfortably as he would speak to a trusted friend. "Father," he prayed, "the hour has come . . . "

Thirty-three years old. Facing certain death. On the last night of His life, as He bowed to pray, Jesus waited to cry out to God on His own behalf until after He had prayed for His disciples. The great high priest, who would both present and become the sacrifice for sin, set aside the anguish in His own soul and assumed His priestly duties by praying for His disciples. He was about to bear their sins in His own body and face the wrath of God in their place. He was about to suffer physical pain and the anguish of being forsaken by His Father. Still, before He cried out to God on His own behalf, asking for the cup to be taken from Him, He prayed what we call today His high priestly prayer, making petition for all whom the Father had given Him—His present and future disciples.

We have already discussed the spiritual discipline of prayer as one of the activities God will use to conform us to the image of His Son. Sadly, this is a discipline too often neglected by task-driven, self-sufficient men. For some reason, it seems, women are more disposed to the duty of prayer. How often have we heard the testimony of a prodigal who has returned to faith in Christ, where he talks about a faithful mother or grandmother who prayed for him daily while he was in rebellion against God? Rarely, to our shame, do we hear of the faithfulness of a praying father.

In the same way that the prophet speaks to the people on behalf of God, the priest has the responsibility and privilege to speak to God on behalf of his people. The ministry of heavenly intercession for those entrusted to his care is a critical part of his calling as a priest. It's not that his wife does not have access to the throne of grace herself; she has the same privileges in the heavenly courts as her husband. The Bible teaches that all believers are part of "a royal priesthood" (1 Pet. 2:9), and as we have pointed out, there is no intermediary between man and God except for the man Christ Jesus (see 1 Tim. 2:5).

Still, it is the responsibility of the priest to oversee and to spiritually shepherd his flock. If a man aspires to be a godly husband, he will assume responsibility for the spiritual condition of his wife. If a husband will love and serve his wife as Christ loves His Church, then the intercessory prayer of Christ in John 17 becomes a model for how a priestly husband can intercede on behalf of his wife.

Petition 1: Glorify God

In the same way that the prayer Jesus spoke during the Sermon on the Mount, commonly called the Lord's Prayer, is a pattern for how we are to pray, so the high priestly prayer in John 17 is a pattern for how a husband can regularly intercede for his wife. The first thing you notice as you read through the prayer is that Jesus begins by praying that God would be glorified by the events that were about to take place (see v. 1). His beginning focus for intercession was what the Westminster Catechism calls "the chief end of man." He prayed that His own triumph over death and sin would ultimately bring glory to His Father.

Too often we rush into the throne room of God and begin blurting out our petitions, either on our own behalf or on behalf of others, without first stopping to remind ourselves of the One in whose presence we stand! Like Jesus, our lives should be consumed by a desire to see God glorified, for His name to be hallowed and for His will to be done in all things. I remember hearing someone say once that the idea of glorifying God—in more modern terms—simply means to brag on Him. Our actions, our words and even our thoughts should all direct the attention of those around us to the majesty and glory that He is due.

A husband, then, should begin his petition for his wife, expressing to God that his desire for her is first and foremost that God would be glorified in and through her life. Above all else, that he might ask God, on her behalf, to see the image of Christ revealed in her. He may pray for her happiness, for her safety and health, or for God to grant her peace in the midst of a difficult circumstance. Those prayers are to rest on the foundation that what he ultimately wants for her is that which brings glory to God.

Husbands are notorious "fixers" when it comes to their wives. If our wives face a difficult trial, we feel a sense of responsibility to rescue them from their distress. In doing so, however, we can find ourselves interfering with the sanctifying work of God in their lives. If God uses suffering to produce perseverance, character and hope (see Rom. 5:3-4), we need to be sensitive to the work of the Holy Spirit in our wives' lives, so as not to interrupt His refining process. The same holds true for our intercessory prayers. We are invited through prayer and petition to present our requests to God (see Phil. 4:6), but we yield those petitions and desires to the ultimate goal of our lives—the glory of God.

Petition 2: Grow in Knowledge

Jesus' second petition in His high priestly prayer was for His disciples to know God (see v. 3). Our lifetime pursuit as believers should be to grow in our knowledge of Christ. Listen to how the apostle Paul prayed in Romans 11:33: "Oh, the depth of the riches of the wisdom and knowledge of God! How unsearchable his judgments, and his paths beyond tracing out!" (NIV). The same apostle prayed for the Philippians "that your love may abound more and more in knowledge and depth of insight" (1:9, NIV). For the Colossians he prayed "that you may live a life worthy of the Lord and may please him in every way: bearing fruit in every good work, growing in the knowledge of God" (1:10, NIV). These verses can be prayed back to God as a petition for our wives. For example, we might pray that her love would abound more and more as she grows in her knowledge of God and her depth of insight.

There is a critical difference between *knowledge about God* and *knowledge of God*. Knowledge about God, according to the Bible, puffs people up, making them arrogant and proud. Today, there are many students of Scripture whose minds are filled with a knowledge about God but whose hearts remain far from Him. In his classic book *Knowing God*, J. I. Packer says that "interest in theology, and knowledge about God, and the capacity to think clearly and talk well on Christian themes, is not at all the same thing as knowing Him."[4]

Knowing God involves an intimate love relationship. When the King James translators of the Bible said that Adam knew Eve, they did not mean to imply that he simply learned some new things about her! That phrase describes the growing intimate relationship between husband and wife, where the two are continually becoming one in body, soul and spirit. Although the sexual overtones are obviously absent, the idea of knowing God reflects the same kind of body, soul and spirit intimacy that is pictured for us in marriage. That's the kind of relationship a husband should be praying for his wife to have with Christ—to be more in love with and devoted to Christ than she is to her own husband.

Petition 3: Hold Fast to the Faith

Jesus also prayed that God would protect His followers (see v. 11). In applying this to how we might intercede for our wives, we might immediately think of her physical security as she walks to her car in the parking lot at the mall or as she drives the kids to soccer practice in the middle of rush-hour traffic. While there is nothing wrong with praying for physical safety, the focus of the Lord's prayer was not for the protection of His disciples. In fact, history and tradition indicate that nearly all those who heard this prayer for protection would ultimately die a painful martyr's death. Only the apostle John lived to an old age, dying years later in Ephesus.

Jesus knew what lay ahead for His disciples. He knew that Peter was about to deny even knowing Him. He knew that Peter and John would wind up in jail for preaching about the Resurrection. He knew that Paul would face constant danger and be stoned, beaten with rods, shipwrecked and put in prison, all for preaching the gospel (see 2 Cor. 11:23-27). He was not praying that Peter, John or Paul would escape the hardships they faced, but instead that God would protect them from despair, discouragement and faithlessness in the middle of their trials that lay ahead.

Therefore, we should pray that our wives would be women who hold fast to their faith, even in the midst of difficult times or of persecution. Our prayer of protection should be aimed not so much at their physical safety, but, as Peter points out, we are to "rejoice that you participate in the sufferings of Christ, so that you may be overjoyed when his glory is revealed" (1 Pet. 4:13, *NIV*).

We can use Psalm 121 as a guide for our prayers of protection: "Lord, do not let my wife's foot slip. Watch over her. Be the shade at her right hand. Keep her from all harm. Watch over her life, in her coming and going, both now and forevermore."

Petition 4: Reflect Holiness

Next, Jesus prays that His followers will be holy, sanctified by the truth of God's Word (see v. 17). This may be hard for a husband to pray for his wife, for often her life reflects a higher commitment to holiness than his own! It sometimes seems that for some reason, she does not face the same moral temptations we face as men. As our sinless Savior, Jesus had the moral authority to pray for our sanctification. A husband may feel he lacks that same authority because of his own struggle against the lust of the flesh, the lust of the eyes and the boastful pride of life (see 1 John 2:16).

We should not be deterred. First, if the prayer for our wife's sanctification calls us up short, it should challenge us again to lead morally

disciplined lives in our own service to Christ. Self-examination is a necessary part of the ministry of intercession, lest we prove to be hypocrites
and Pharisees. One reason God invites us to pray for one another and to
intercede on behalf of our wives is so that He can use the discipline of
intercessory prayer as a means of speaking to our hearts about our own
walk with Christ.

Additionally, we need to understand that while there is a moral
dimension to the biblical idea of holiness and sanctification, the primary meaning of both words is that we be men and women who are useful—set apart for service to Christ. Being morally pure, and reflecting a
standard of righteousness, is part of what makes us useful, and it is certainly not to be overlooked or minimized. When a man prays that God
would sanctify his wife, he is asking Him to make her useful in His service today.

Petition 5: Draw Close

Jesus then prayed that His followers would be brought to complete unity
(see v. 23). Here, we have an opportunity as husbands to pray for our
wives in an area that touches the core of how God designed them as
women. Women tend more than men to be more oriented toward relationships, and the prayer for unity is a plea to God that we would be of
one heart and one mind in our relationships with others in the Body of
Christ.

Here is an opportunity for a husband to intercede for what ought to
be his wife's primary relationship—her relationship with him. He can
pray that they would continue to draw closer to each other, rather than
yielding to the natural drifting apart that all couples experience in marriage. When he experiences conflict with his wife, he can pray for God to
intervene. John Yates, in his helpful book *How a Man Prays for His Family*,
encourages husbands to diligently pray that God would move them
toward unity in their marriage:

> If your wife has irritating habits or attitudes it is possible that
> you—her husband, lover, supporter—are not the right person to
> bring about those changes in her life. But you can, as a prayer

partner, work on these things by talking to God about them and seeking His help on her behalf.[5]

A husband also needs to intercede for unity in his wife's relationships with other women in the Body of Christ. Today, however, the cry for unity among believers is often misguided. It is a unity founded exclusively on a person's profession of faith in Christ. As long as a person claims to have been born again or says "I love Jesus," we are implored to "tear down the walls" and embrace that person as our brother or sister in Christ. John 17 is often cited as proof that Jesus wants us all to be one.

It is important to notice, however, that Jesus' prayer for the unity of His disciples followed His prayer that they be sanctified in truth. The only basis for true unity is the "one faith, one Lord, one baptism" unity that binds our hearts together in a common understanding of the gospel. While we might as believers charitably disagree on important issues, such as whether infants or adults should be baptized, we must be united around the essence of the Christian faith, the gospel of Christ.

In the seventeenth century, Puritan pastor Richard Baxter suggested a helpful formula for articulating the boundaries for our unity: "In necessary things, unity; in doubtful things, liberty; in all things, charity."[6]

A husband's prayer for his wife in this area, then, ought to be founded on her understanding of the gospel. Her unity with other believers in Christ (even with him!) should be centered in the "necessary things" to which Baxter alluded. We can pray that our wives would find companions and soul mates who share not only their faith in Christ but also convictions about how to live as godly women and as godly wives. We can pray that the enemy would not disrupt those relationships, and that when there are conflicts or hurt feelings, she will follow the Lord's instructions in Matthew 5:23-24:

Therefore if you are presenting your offering at the altar, and there remember that your brother has something against you, leave your offering there before the altar and go; first be reconciled to your brother, and then come and present your offering.

Your wife needs the strength that comes from solid relationships with others in the Body of Christ who share a common faith, what the apostle Peter called "a faith of the same kind as ours" (2 Pet. 1:1). A husband ought to be interceding for her, asking God to knit her heart with other women.

Petition 6: Remain Faithful

Jesus' final petition in John 17 is for us to be with Him, beholding His glory (see v. 24). Today—right now—the Lord is seated at the right hand of God, interceding on our behalf (see Heb. 7:25) and preparing a place for us (see John 14:1-2) to spend eternity with those who are His own. As husbands, we can pray on our wife's behalf that our Lord would return quickly and take us to be with Him.

In Matthew 25, Jesus tells His followers about 10 young women—virgins—who were waiting for their bridegroom to come. Five of the women stayed ready, keeping their wicks trimmed and their lamps filled with oil. The other five women proved themselves to be faithless. They had expressed some initial interest in the bridegroom, but as the day of his return continued to be delayed, they lost interest in his coming. When he came, those who were ready were swept off to the wedding feast, while the foolish virgins were left behind. They came knocking on the door, begging to be let in, but were turned away by the bridegroom, who announced, "I never knew you."

A true disciple of Christ is one who proves faithful to the end. Jesus ended His high priestly prayer for us by asking God that we might be with Him in heaven, beholding Him in His glory and majesty. In exercising his priestly responsibilities, a husband ought to also pray for his wife, that she would persevere in her faith and so might prove the reality of her profession of faith in Christ. At the same time, he can join his own heart with the heart of his master by praying that the wedding feast might take place soon.

In Closing

Following Jesus' pattern of intercession in John 17, then, a husband should pray for his wife that she would glorify God; that she would know Him;

that God would keep her safe in Him; that she would be set apart for His service; that she would be one with Him and with other godly women; and that she would stay faithful to the end. In doing so, he will fulfill his responsibility as her priestly intercessor.

I spoke recently with one husband who had attended a FamilyLife Marriage Conference with his wife. The two of them had been separated for nearly four months. Although both the man and his wife were angry and bitter toward each other, they attended the conference to see if they could find any help for their struggling marriage.

The conference had a profound spiritual impact on both of them. They began to understand the issues that had pushed them toward isolation. They also heard the practical things taught in Scripture that would lead them back toward intimacy. For this husband, one of those practical steps involved a daily time of prayer and study with his wife.

By the time I met this husband, it had been nearly a year since he'd initiated that regular activity with his wife. "Since the conference," he told me, "we have started each day with a devotional time together. We read a passage of Scripture and we pray together. That one simple step has had a profound impact on our marriage." He had learned how to be the priest that God—and his wife—wanted him to be.

A priestly husband leads his wife in worship, reminds her of the good news of the gospel and intercedes for her just as Christ intercedes for His Bride, the Church.

PointstoConsider

1. What factors have shaped your view of what it means for a man to be "head" of his wife? Describe some of the role models you have observed (including your father, if appropriate).

2. What do the following verses tell you about a man's role in marriage?

- Ephesians 5:22-29
- 1 Corinthians 11:3
- Colossians 3:18-19

3. Three different aspects of a man's headship are discussed in this chapter. What do you think it means for a husband to act as "priest" in his family?

4. Is it difficult for you to consider the responsibility of leading your family in worship and prayer?

5. What is a step you could take during the next week to begin leading your family in this way?

6. Read through Christ's prayer in John 17. How is this a model for ways a man can pray for his wife and his family?

CHAPTER 7

THE HUSBAND WHO HEARS FROM GOD

Every governor of a family ought to look upon himself as obligated to act in three
capacities: as a prophet to instruct; as a priest to pray for and with; and as a king to
govern, direct and provide for them. It is true, indeed that the latter of these, their
kingly office, they are not so frequently deficient in . . . but as for the former,
their priestly and prophetic offices . . . they care for no such thing.

GEORGE WHITEFIELD, "THE GREAT DUTY OF FAMILY RELIGION"

It was a Friday afternoon, late in the workday, when my friend Phil received
an urgent call from his wife. "You need to come home right now," she told
him. Phil looked at his computer at the task that was almost complete,
glanced at his watch and wondered about the urgency in his wife's voice.
It was not like Christy to call him at work and to insist that he come home.

"I'll have to come in on Saturday to finish up," he told her, making sure she had weighed whether the need of the moment could wait a few hours until he arrived home. She understood. She needed to talk to him. She'd been thinking about it all day, and it wouldn't wait.

Phil and Christy had been married three years and had recently welcomed a daughter as an addition to their family. Something that day had triggered a need in Christy's soul, and she felt compelled by God to address the matter with her husband. Phil told me later that he arrived home to a wife who properly and appropriately rebuked him.

"I need you," Christy told him, "to teach me, to disciple me in the faith." Although the two had grown up in Christian homes, had been in church all their lives and had attended a Christian college together, Christy still had an unmet longing for her husband to teach her the Scriptures and to nurture her in her relationship with God. "You know so much," she told him. "I need you to lead me."

Phil said it was a wake-up call for him as a husband. Christy was not nagging her husband to add one more duty to his list of husbandly chores. She was prophetically calling him to be the husband God wanted him to be and that she longed for him to be. She was calling him to fulfill his responsibility as a prophet.

As he told me that story, I flashed back almost two decades, to the time early in our marriage when I told Mary Ann I wanted to teach a Bible study in our home. I knew that the best way for me to be disciplined in my own study of God's Word was for me to have a teaching assignment that would force me to dig into the Scriptures. Although I had only been a Christian for a few years, I was hungry to know the Word and to teach others.

There was one problem with my Bible study idea. I wasn't sure where I was going to get any students. We invited a few friends to join us at our home on a Tuesday night to begin a study in the book of Romans. I typed an outline for the lesson and made enough copies to hand out to anyone who came.

The first knock at the door came a few minutes after seven on Tuesday. My friend Larry stood at the door with his Bible in hand. I ushered him in, got him a Coke and we made small talk as we waited for others.

By about 7:30, it was clear that all who were coming had arrived. We began our study of Romans that night with a teacher and two students—Larry and my wife. Undeterred, I plowed ahead with an introduction to Paul's epistle.

Our Tuesday-night study continued for the next several months, as the three of us worked our way through Paul's masterpiece like Sunday-afternoon hikers trying to scale Mount McKinley. There were lots of questions raised that none of us knew the answers to, but the discipline of that weekly study kept me faithfully in the Scriptures.

I'll never forget one particular evening when our study brought us face-to-face with one of the most controversial doctrines in the Bible—the doctrine of predestination and election. It might have been at chapter 8, when we arrived at verse 29 and found that "whom He foreknew, He also predestined to become conformed to the image of His Son."

I found myself wrestling with the implications of the passage. Any time I had run up against the idea of election in the past, I had been able to easily overlook it or conclude that somehow God chooses us after we choose Him. Now the more I poured over the text, the more I had to conclude that predestination meant something greater than that.

That evening, with a growing sense of confidence and boldness, I explained to my wife and my friend Larry that we did not choose God, but He chose us. In our living room that night, I opened the same can of worms that has been the source of wars, church splits and division for the past 2,000 years. I was a three-year-old tinkering with dynamite. I had no idea of the explosion that was about to occur.

Halfway through the study, Mary Ann became so frustrated and so angry that she got up and left the room. It was an awkward moment as I sat with Larry, wondering whether she was coming back or whether I should ask him to hold on a minute while I went to talk to my wife. I finally decided that Larry and I would press ahead. The two of us finished the study alone that evening.

Mary Ann and I laugh together about that story today, but at the time it was no laughing matter for an insecure, young husband. Now as I thought about my friend Phil being challenged by his wife to take the lead and to teach her the Scriptures, I had to wonder if he might be in for an evening or two like Mary Ann and I had experienced in our study of Romans!

A part of the headship responsibility every husband bears is the call to be a prophet. In its simplest definition, the term means, "one who hears from God" or "one who speaks for God." The prophet of God has always performed the simple act of hearing and speaking the word of the Lord.

Before the close of the canon of Scripture, prophets would receive the word of the Lord supernaturally. Whether the Lord spoke audibly to them, sent angels with messages or simply impressed His word on their hearts, the prophets of God were men and women who declared the will of God to others. Sometimes they would prove their prophetic vocation by predicting a future event or telling accurately something they could only know through divine revelation. In John 4, for example, when Jesus told the woman at the well that she had been married five times and was now living with a man who was not her husband, she responded by saying, "Sir, I perceive that You are a prophet" (v. 19). He knew things only God would know, and so He established His prophetic office.

The predictive nature of the prophetic office was largely given to confirm for the people the trustworthiness of the prophet. Without a revealed canon of Scripture to use as a test of truth, people had to determine the veracity of a prophet on the basis of his or her knowledge of hidden things. But the primary function of the prophet was never to tell the future. A quick survey of the prophetic literature in the Bible, from Isaiah to Malachi, will show the chief responsibility of the prophetic office was proclamation. Their message was generally the same. They reminded God's people of His providential love and care for them. They revealed His plan of salvation. When Israel was in rebellion, paying no attention to God, the prophet bore the assignment of announcing God's impending judgment for their sin and calling them to cry out to Him for salvation.

Although the prophetic office is fulfilled in Christ, the prophetic function continues in the home, the Church and in the community. Today, a prophet does not need to rely on a supernatural revelation to proclaim God's truth. The Scriptures provide us with the completed, objective revelation of God for men. A prophet today is one who speaks on the authority of God's Word, calling men and women to repent of sin, to find their salvation in Christ and to find their rest in His unfailing love and care.

Author and counselor Dan Allender offers a helpful definition of what it means to serve Christ as a prophet today:

> He is a bearer of the word of God, a spokesman for righteousness, a poet of hope. . . . The true prophet disturbs and invites the heart to return to godly worship. In fact, the prophet is a servant of the church who stands outside the church in order to invite those who appear to be in it to return to true worship."[1]

With this view of a prophet in mind, the apostle Paul calls men to "pursue love, yet desire earnestly spiritual gifts, but especially that you may prophesy" (1 Cor. 14:1).

The Prophetic Husband

The prophetic role has been all but abandoned in the modern Church. A Christian husband today who did not observe his father exercising his prophetic duties stumbles into marriage without any model of how to be properly prophetic in his relationship with his wife. Although he may lack a flesh-and-blood model of how to fill the prophetic office, the Scriptures are full of examples, especially the example of the One who perfectly executed His prophetic duties.

Here are the marks of a prophetic husband.

He Hears from God

The prophet bears the Word of God. Before he can speak on God's behalf, he must clearly hear the Word of God so that he might faithfully pass it on to his wife and his children.

The author of Hebrews reminds us that God "spoke long ago to the fathers in the prophets in many portions and in many ways" (1:1).

Without the Bible as a reference, prophets relied on hearing directly from God—in dreams, in visions, through an audible voice or through an impression in their spirit.

Today, we have the completed revelation of God to man in the pages of the Bible. Dreams, visions and audible voices are not the ordinary ways God chooses to speak to us today. He has provided us with a more certain, more trustworthy record of His Word to His people. A prophet today does not need to hope for "a word from the Lord" about a particular subject, because he has the sure Word of God as his guide.

To hear from God today, a husband must be diligent to equip himself as a student of the Scriptures. Douglas Wilson, in his book *Reforming Marriage*, says, "a man may not be a vocational theologian, but in his home he must be the resident theologian. The apostle Paul, when he is urging women to keep silent in the church, tells them that 'if they desire to learn anything, let them ask their own husbands at home' (1 Cor. 14:35). The tragedy is that many modern women have to wonder why the Bible says they should have to ask their husbands. 'He doesn't know.' But a husband must be prepared to answer his wife's doctrinal questions, and if he cannot, then he must be prepared to study so that he can remedy the deficiency."[2]

We think of a prophet as one who proclaims God's truth. First and foremost, he hears from God so that he can proclaim the truth accurately. A husband who attempts to speak on God's behalf should tremble at the assignment. False prophets in the Old Testament were stoned. The New Testament warns us to "be diligent to present yourself approved to God as a workman who does not need to be ashamed, accurately handling the word of truth" (2 Tim. 2:15). The spiritual disciplines of a godly man begin with reading, studying, meditating on and memorizing the Word of God.

He Establishes a Doctrinal Foundation for His Home

We live in an age when doctrine is somehow viewed as negative. You have probably heard a preacher say at some point something like this: "You don't need doctrine, you just need Jesus!" Doctrine is viewed as rigid, stuffy, boring, divisive and almost antithetical to the cause of Christ.

In truth, there is no understanding of the Scriptures or of who Jesus is without some understanding of theology and doctrine. In a discussion once with a friend who was down on doctrine, I asked the simple question: "Who is this Jesus in whom you claim to believe?" My friend was puzzled by such an obvious question. "He's the Son of God, the Savior of the world!" he replied. "No, no, no," I protested. "I don't want theology! Don't give me that doctrinal stuff! Just tell me who Jesus is!"

The point quickly became obvious to my friend. Anytime we attempt to express basic truths of the Christian faith, we are dealing with doctrine. "Theology" is a word that literally means "the study of God." Rather than ignoring theological and doctrinal issues, dismissing them as foolish or unnecessary, a husband should find himself wrestling with the issues raised in Scripture. He must determine for his wife and his family what is right and true.

Immediately, some women might bristle at the idea that their husbands should decide for them how to understand and interpret the Scriptures. In fact, if a husband is faithful to study, a wife can feel secure that God will speak to him, since God himself has placed her husband in the prophetic office in their home. Her husband will not be infallible in his understanding of Scripture. He should seek to learn from his wife also as she studies the Word of God for herself. But their home is to be founded on the husband's clear statement of conviction and belief about what the Bible teaches. He should establish a confessional standard for his home.

Years ago, a husband would assume the responsibility for catechizing his household. Typically, his wife had been raised in the Church and would come into the marriage already rooted in a proper understanding of the Word. His primary responsibility then involved the training of his children. He would lead them in memorizing long doctrinal statements that served to ground them in a basic understanding of the Scriptures.

Only a generation ago, we dumbed down that catechizing standard to include memorization of John 3:16, the Lord's Prayer, the Apostles' Creed and "Jesus Loves Me." Today, in most evangelical churches, we've determined that the Apostles' Creed and the Lord's Prayer are no longer necessary. Those doctrinal standards that were supposed to protect us from error have been left in the dust, and the Church has us reaping the harvest of theological illiteracy in the pew.

Douglas Wilson astutely blames husbands for this theological breakdown. "The evangelical world," he writes, "is throwing away its theological heritage because of doctrinal faithlessness in Christian homes. It is true that pulpits across our country are filled with a swamp and morass of anecdotes, sentimentalist yawp, yippy-skippy worship, and make-it-up-as-you-go-along theology; but the heads of Christian homes have been willing to have it so. As the expectations for men in the evangelical world have gotten lower, men have not objected—they have breathed a sigh of relief."[3]

There will undoubtedly be times when a husband and wife disagree on how to understand a particular passage. They may find themselves divided on matters of doctrine. They may have been raised in different denominations, and may still have patterns or preferences that are part of that heritage.

Here, a husband must use great wisdom, skill and sensitivity in loving and spiritually leading his wife. What are the issues involved? If they are simply a matter of individual preference, then don't make a big deal out of them. Move on. Are they essential? Then with gentleness and grace look together at what the Scriptures teach so that you and your wife can hold on to what C. S. Lewis described as "mere Christianity." Be patient and look to the Lord with your hearts.

Here is a biblical principle that you can wisely apply to deal with doctrinal differences you might have with your wife. The apostle Paul had heard about doctrinal divisions in the Church at Rome. There, the debate centered around dietary restrictions and whether to observe certain days as holy or set apart (see Rom. 14:1-17). His conclusion? "Let us not judge one another anymore," he said, "but rather determine this—not to put an obstacle or a stumbling block in a brother's way. For the kingdom of God is not eating and drinking, but righteousness and peace and joy in the Holy Spirit" (vv. 13,17).

Husbands who fill the prophetic office will have to use Paul's wisdom when there is division. They should never compromise in lovingly holding to the essentials of the faith. They should also allow for liberty in nonessential areas, seeking to promote "righteousness and peace and joy in the Holy Spirit."

John Calvin referred to a prophet as a supplier of useful doctrine. In addition to hearing from God, a husband should fill that role in his home.

He Faithfully Proclaims the Truth of God

On long drives, late at night, when the kids are sleeping in the back, Mary Ann and I have found ourselves reviewing things we've learned together in church. Or we rehearse concepts I've picked up from reading or listening to tapes. "What is the Latin phrase that means 'at once sinful and justified'?" I'll ask.

"I'm too tired to play this," she'll say.

"I'm too tired not to play!" I'll coax her. "Help me stay awake."

Together, we'll mentally review books of the Bible, or we'll toss out a verse and see if the other one knows where it's found. We may listen to a teaching tape and wind up discussing what we've heard. As the drive wears on, the game will usually deteriorate to the point where I'm asking questions like: "Name three hits by the Lovin' Spoonful."

In their fantasies of what it will be like to be married, many young Christian women dream of a husband who will read a devotional with them over coffee at the breakfast table and read the Scriptures to them as they go to sleep at night. Meanwhile, many young Christian men are having a different dream of a woman who will watch *Monday Night Football* with them!

The truth is, for many Christian men, the idea of some formal time of Bible study or instruction is in their top 10 list of threatening activities. We feel inadequate and unsure of ourselves. We're not sure how to do it or what to say when we're finished. We're not eloquent like the pastor. We're afraid we'll be exposed for what we don't know, for the shallowness of our own spirituality. Or we fear being convicted of hypocrisy by a wife who knows too well that we don't always practice what we preach.

As a result, most Christian husbands have abandoned any attempt at trying to lead their wives in any kind of informal study of the Scriptures. They may make a stab at some kind of family devotions once the children are old enough to sit still, but as the kids squirm or stare out the window, most men throw in the towel and give up the whole idea altogether.

The prophetic call for a husband is a call to provide spiritual nourishment for his wife. Puritan pastor Samuel Davies made the point that Christian husbands have accepted the responsibility of providing for the material needs of their wives, as 1 Timothy 5:8 commands them to do. Davies then asked why we are so quick to care for those material needs, which are not eternal, while we ignore the spiritual needs of our wives and our families, which will endure forever. In our era, driven by material gain and workaholism, it's a sobering question.

Most of us husbands are intimidated by the task of proclaiming God's truth, because we expect too much of ourselves in the process. We think we need to prepare a daily devotional with three points and a poem. If we read a chapter from the Bible, we think we have to have some wise insight into the text when we're finished, as if the Word isn't powerful or capable of explaining itself. Mostly, we don't want to blow our cover and expose our own lack of understanding of the deep things of God, especially in front of our wives.

In reality, our wives already know what's lacking. We won't be exposing much. A husband needs to muster his courage and take the initiative to regularly call his wife and his family to the Scriptures as their source of life and truth. He doesn't have to rely on his own insights or creativity. There are tools, like Dennis and Barbara Rainey's devotional *Moments Together for Couples*, or the daily devotional magazine *Tabletalk*, produced by Ligonier Ministries, that a man can read aloud with his wife. He can stand on the shoulders of others as he seeks to establish his marriage on the truth of the Scriptures.

He Confronts Sin and Calls His Wife to Repentance

Perhaps this was the most difficult assignment facing a biblical prophet. Over and over again in the Scriptures, we see the prophets of God pronouncing judgment on God's people for their idolatry, apostasy and faithlessness to the law of God. Nowhere is this more vivid than in the prophetic ministry of Jesus as He wept over the sins of the nation of

Israel, pronouncing His own divine judgment on them:

> Jerusalem, Jerusalem, who kills the prophets and stones those
> who are sent to her! How often I wanted to gather your children
> together, the way a hen gathers her chicks under her wings, and
> you were unwilling. Behold, your house is being left to you des-
> olate! For I say to you, from now on you shall not see Me until
> you say, "Blessed is He who comes in the name of the Lord!"
> (Matt. 23:37-39).

We often picture the prophets as angry, but the example of Jesus is
that of a weeping prophet, who mourns over sin and who grieves for the
chastening and judgment that will follow. So should it be for a husband
who may on occasion be called on by God to confront his wife about her
sin.

A husband may shirk this aspect of his prophetic responsibilities for
several reasons. First, confronting sin and calling a wife to repentance
will likely rock the domestic boat. Jonah was a reluctant prophet because
the people of Nineveh were known for their harsh treatment of their enemies. Just outside the city walls was a huge tower of human heads that
had been severed in battle. Jonah had to wonder how his message of
judgment from God was going to go over with these barbarians. In the
same way, a husband may decide not to confront his wife about some
sinful behavior on her part, because he doesn't want to make her angry.
Like Jonah, however, he needs to obey God's call regardless of how his
wife will respond.

Second, a husband might fail to confront his wife about some
wrongdoing because he has a soft view of what it means to love her.
Pointing out sin seems harsh and judgmental, not loving. Our example
here is Christ, who loves us too much to overlook our sin. The same
weeping prophet who pronounced judgment on Israel comes to us today
by His Holy Spirit to convict us of our sin and to lead us to righteousness. If we begin to understand the consequences of sin for ourselves and
for future generations, we will not think it loving to ignore or overlook
our wives' ongoing patterns of sinful behavior.

A prophet may also feel hypocritical pointing out the speck in his wife's eye when he is aware of the log of his own sin. But Jesus' instructions were clear in this regard. The real hypocrisy is in confronting your wife about her sin without first taking care of your own sin. "First," Jesus said, "take the log out of your own eye, and then you will see clearly to take the speck out of your brother's eye" (Matt. 7:5). Some husbands may avoid their prophetic responsibilities because they don't want to face their own sin.

The pattern provided by the Savior here is not to be passed over. A husband who sets off to "fix" his wife without first doing his own self-examination is both arrogant and foolish. If he is not willing to humbly acknowledge his own struggles with sin, he is not fit to help his wife with hers. If he's not sure about his own sins, all he needs to do is ask his wife. She is undoubtedly very aware of what they are!

The pattern for confronting a sinful brother (or wife) is found in Galatians 6:1-2. Paul writes, "Brethren, even if anyone is caught in any trespass, you who are spiritual, restore such a one in a spirit of gentleness; each one looking to yourself, so that you too will not be tempted. Bear one another's burdens, and thereby fulfill the law of Christ." First, examine your own heart to make sure you're not ensnared in the same sin. Second, seek to restore the other person in his or her walk with Christ and relationship with you. Third, confront with gentleness, not with a spirit of judgment or condemnation. Fourth, be ready to bear the other person's burden as he or she seeks freedom from the bondage of a besetting sin.

Imagine a man whose wife watches three hours of soap operas every afternoon. Not only is he convinced that the activity is wasting, not redeeming, her time (see Eph. 5:16), but he also is concerned about the ungodly content of the programs. He may be seeing patterns develop in her life that he believes are a result of her three-hour daily attachment to the TV (see Rom. 12:2).

The husband is responsible to confront his wife about her sin. But first, he needs to examine his own life and determine if there are activities in which he is involved that violate the same biblical standards. Is he wasting time each day surfing the Internet or watching ESPN? Does he rationalize his own habit—"I need to unwind after a hard day at work"—while being concerned about her actions? Or is he letting his mind dwell on unwholesome or unprofitable thoughts by watching movies or prime-time shows that have as much or more in them to be concerned about?

Once he has struggled with his own heart and can see the fruit of his repentance (a prolonged period where he has replaced sinful patterns with spiritual disciplines), he needs next to make sure his motives are pure. Is his goal to see his wife sanctified in Christ? Or is there any vindictive or judgmental spirit at work in his heart?

Is he able to approach his wife with the right spirit, one that shows humility and love, rather than condemnation? Is his heart broken by the knowledge of how her behavior grieves the Savior?

Finally, is he ready to stand with her, bearing her burdens? Perhaps the issue is not really the soap operas at all. Maybe they are symptoms of a much deeper issue such as a heart that is in rebellion to the will and the Word of God. The husband must be ready, as a fellow struggler, to help his wife understand the issues of her soul that draw her to the soap operas. He may even come to find out that her own sinful patterns are a result of the poor job he has been doing as a lover, in failing to meet her deep longing for relationship.

It's easy to see why many husbands would rather not confront sinful behavior they see in their wives. (I include myself in their number!) Most books on how to have a happy marriage don't suggest that confrontation over sin is one of the keys, but we are reminded in Proverbs that the wounds of a friend are faithful (see 27:6). If our goal is the glory of God, happiness in marriage will take a backseat to the higher calling of helping a sister in Christ be conformed to His likeness. The hard task of prophetic confrontation is a necessary part of working toward that goal.

He Encourages His Wife with the Truth of God's Love

The prophets of God in the Old Testament have gained a reputation. We see them today as men and women who stood fearlessly in the face of apostasy, announcing judgment and calling God's people to repent. When we consider our role as prophetic husbands, we may imagine ourselves as men who constantly confront our wives, pointing out her faults and challenging her to change.

It would be wrong, I believe, for us to assume that the men and women raised up by God as His prophets were sour, angry faultfinders. They took no pleasure in announcing God's coming judgment or calling for repentance. We should not imagine that these were social misfits who didn't care that their message would be unpopular or that they would be scorned and ridiculed. Jonah was a reluctant prophet. Jeremiah wept as he delivered his message. They fulfilled their duties out of obedience, not because doing so was easy or fun.

But their message always involved more than coming judgment or a call to repentance. They were continually reminding the people of God's faithfulness, His love and His mercy. Some of the most wonderful revelations of God's character come from the prophets:

> Do not fear, for I have redeemed you; I have called you by name; you are Mine! When you pass through the waters, I will be with you; and through the rivers, they will not overflow you. When you walk through the fire, you will not be scorched, nor will the flame burn you (Isa. 43:1-2).

> I have loved you with an everlasting love; therefore I have drawn you with lovingkindness (Jer. 31:3).

> I will heal their apostasy, I will love them freely, for My anger has turned away from them (Hos. 14:4).

> Who is a God like You, who pardons iniquity and passes over the rebellious act of the remnant of His possession? He does not retain His anger forever, because He delights in unchanging love (Mic. 7:18).

> The LORD your God is in your midst, a victorious warrior. He will exult over you with joy, He will be quiet in His love, He will rejoice over you with shouts of joy (Zeph. 3:17).

The sober message of the prophets was one of coming judgment for Israel. Yet in the midst of that message came the prophetic reminders of God's love, His grace, His mercy and His compassion. The prophet was a messenger of hope.

Most wives don't need a constant reminder of their own sin, especially from their husbands. They are painfully aware of their shortcomings and their failures. Instead, they need to be reminded of God's forgiveness when they stumble. They need to hear again that His mercies are new every morning (see Lam. 3:22-23). They long for encouragement.

Look again at the five examples of positive encouragement listed above. When was the last time you reminded your wife that God is with her, and that He will take care of her in the face of difficulties and adversity (see Isa. 43:1-2)? Or that God's love is an everlasting love, no matter what (see Jer. 31:3)? Or that God loves her, and His anger is turned away (see Hos. 14:4)? Or that He is a forgiving God (see Mic. 7:18)? Or that He rejoices over her with shouts of joy (see Zeph. 3:17)?

Those prophetic messages from God are like cool water to a thirsty soul. A husband ought to make it his assignment to daily remind his wife of God's unconditional love for her. He needs to encourage her regularly that God is cheering for her!

In a word, your wife needs to grow in her understanding of God's *grace*.

The husband who concentrates on confronting sin has missed the mark. As we speak for God, we need to make sure that His message of grace and love is coming through loud and clear.

In Closing

The prophetic responsibilities outlined in this chapter are one part of the serious role God has called every husband to fulfill. Jesus knew full well that those responsibilities lie down the narrow road. "A prophet is not without honor," Jesus said, "except in his hometown and *among his own relatives and in his own household*" (Mark 6:4, emphasis added). A husband can expect that the faithful execution of his prophetic responsibilities will be hard work. It requires love. It requires patience. It requires serious self-examination. A husband must fulfill his prophetic responsibilities in the power of the Holy Spirit, manifesting the fruit of the Holy Spirit at all times (see Gal. 5:22-23). If he attempts to execute his duties with the arm of the flesh, it will explode in his face, and he'll wind up writing me a nasty letter about how my book is for the birds. Or worse, he may critically damage his relationship with his wife. If a husband doesn't know how to "speak the truth in love," he's not ready as a husband to speak the truth at all.

If your objective in marriage is to have a calm, peaceful, friendly relationship with a woman who trades you domestic chores and sex for a part of your paycheck and domestic security, you can ignore the call of God to be a prophetic husband. But if your goal is a marriage where God is glorified, where each partner is growing in his or her knowledge of the Savior and being sanctified daily by His Spirit, and where two souls are being knit together in true intimacy, it will be necessary for you to assume the prophetic mantle as you lead your wife and family.

PointstoConsider

1. A husband is responsible to listen to God and to call his wife and family to "repent of sin, to find their salvation in Christ and to find their rest in His unfailing love and care." As you look at your family, do you need to call your wife and family to trust in God in some particular situations?
2. In 1 Corinthians 14:35, Paul tells women that "if they desire to learn anything, let them ask their own husbands at home." What does this say about a husband's responsibility in the home?
3. What does 2 Timothy 2:15 say about a man's responsibility? How would you evaluate your ability in "accurately handling the word of truth"?
4. How should you handle a disagreement between you and your wife about an interpretation of a passage in Scripture?
5. Have you and your wife ever studied Scripture together?

- If you have: What works best for you? What makes it difficult for you to do this consistently?
- If you have not: What is preventing you from beginning this discipline within the next week?

6. One important role of Old Testament prophets, and of Jesus during His time here on Earth, was to confront sin and call people to repentance. What makes it difficult for men to assume this responsibility in marriage by confronting sin?

7. Why is it beneficial for you to continually remind your wife about God's unfailing love for her?

8. What are some problems or circumstances in your wife's life right now that might lead her to question God's love for her? How could you encourage her?

CHAPTER 8

THE HUSBAND WHO LOVES AND LEADS

We have seen how a husband is called by God to be both priest and prophet to his wife. Now we come to the discussion of the husband as king—leader of his wife and family. Because that title brings to mind the reign of both corrupt monarchs and noble rulers, I offer a modern fairy tale for husbands that I hope will set the stage for our discussion.

The Tale of the Three Kings

Once upon a time, there lived three kings who ruled over three tiny kingdoms. Their names were King Moe, King Larry and King Rocky I. The possible names King Curly and King Schemp have been rejected, because the third king is the hero of the story, and neither name really fits a hero. The reason King Rocky is noted as Rocky I is to keep the reader from becoming confused with the sequels.

King Moe was known throughout his tiny kingdom as a despot. Although he was very smart and could be very charming when he wanted to be, he was a self-centered king who delighted in exercising the authority he inherited from his father. Many mornings when he awakened, he would summon one of his subjects to his bedside and require that the subject fold back the covers for him so that he might more easily get out of bed. The fact that someone had to climb four flights of stairs to do something he could have easily done himself didn't phase King Moe. He was the king; thus, he was entitled to give orders. And heaven help the servant who might wrinkle the king's bedspread or sheets—she would find herself the object of his furious, uncontrolled wrath.

King Larry was a very different kind of king. Early in his reign, he was widely regarded as a most pleasant king, friendly and well liked by his subjects. He was easygoing and affable, and his kingdom reflected his relaxed and laid-back style. However, as time passed, the subjects in King Larry's kingdom grew restless and frustrated by their ruler. It wasn't that King Larry was wicked or cruel like King Moe, but he just didn't do very much at all. They would report to him that the moat around the castle was in need of repair, and he listened but did nothing about it. When blight destroyed more than half of the wheat crop one year, the subjects looked to the king for help. King Larry didn't know what to do, so he mostly ignored the problem. He would spend his days sitting on his throne with a big bowl of popcorn, watching videos of action movies and early Steve Martin comedies. "My subjects are lucky," he thought to himself. "I'm not a cruel king like King Moe." His frustrated subjects would sometimes feel guilty, wondering if they just expected too much from their leader.

The third tiny kingdom was ruled by King Rocky I. He was not as smart as King Moe or as easygoing as King Larry, but he was a hardworking king who tried to rule his subjects and lead his kingdom as best as he knew how. When there was peace in his kingdom, he would gather

his counselors together for their thoughts on how to improve the quali
ty of life in the kingdom. In wartime, his advisers met daily to provide
him with up-to-date information from the battlefield. On many days, he
would ride into battle himself, offering his own counsel and encouragement to his soldiers. Because King Rocky I was quick to seek counsel,
some mistakenly assumed he ruled by a democratic consensus. This was
not the case. King Rocky I still made the final decisions, even if they were
unpopular and went against the wisdom of his advisors. He was willing
to assume responsibility for unwise decisions (which he made more frequently than one might expect); and he was quick to share the glory
when his plans succeeded. He was not always popular, and his kingdom
had its share of hard times, but he tried to lead his people with wisdom,
and they generally looked to their king with respect and with love.

One night all three kings were watching TV as they settled into bed
in their respective kingdoms, when they heard the theme music for
Nightline. All three kings' ears perked up as Ted Koppel said, "To the outside world, they appear to be three stable and prosperous kingdoms. But
how ready are these kingdoms and their rulers to face an attack from
barbarians? And is there growing unrest among their own subjects?
We'll take an in-depth look tonight on *Nightline*."

After the commercial, King Moe sat up straight in bed as Ted began
to describe what life was like under his rule. He was pleased to hear himself described as a tough, no-nonsense king who ruled with an iron fist.
Ted showed footage of King Moe inspecting the troops, barking out
orders that sent his advisers scurrying off and making long, loud speech-
es to his subjects.

But King Moe was not prepared for what came next. "All is not well
in King Moe's kingdom," Ted said. "While most of his subjects refused
to appear on camera for this report, most of the people we interviewed
were quick to voice their dislike for their leader. He was described almost
universally as arrogant, insecure and a coward. In fact, according to an
ABC News/New York Times poll, 77 percent of King Moe's subjects say
they feel oppressed and 84 percent disapprove of the way he is running
the kingdom. If an invasion were to occur, it is unclear how many of the
king's men might actually begin fighting for the enemy."

King Moe was furious. He rang for his prime minister. "First thing tomorrow, I want you to find out the names of the people who were interviewed and who were polled!" he shouted. "They must be punished. And send word to the general to find out the names of the would-be traitors and have them shot!"

The trembling prime minister stammered, "My king, it will be done as you say. If it pleases the king, may I be so bold to ask, how would you have me respond to questions from the news media?"

"The news media!" the king bellowed.

"Yes, my liege," the prime minister answered. "Already they are calling for your reaction to the program."

A sly smile crept across the face of the king. "You may tell them that their king is not concerned about his approval ratings. He is not interested in being popular." His voice slowly grew louder. "Tell them he is the king, and his commands will be obeyed or else!"

The voice of the king could be heard echoing through the castle. After what seemed like an eternity of silence, the prime minister said in a mousy little voice, "Or else what, sir?"

King Moe, who had been quite pleased with his bellowing, cocked his head to one side and paused. For a minute, the words from the TV flashed back through his mind: "arrogant," "insecure," "a coward." Was it possible?

"Or else," he said slowly, "they will know the wrath of their king as they have never known it before."

King Moe climbed back in his bed, smugly satisfied that he had once again demonstrated his power and authority as king. He might even call that Ted Koppel tomorrow and give him a piece of his mind.

The prime minister scampered from the king's chambers, reviewing his instructions and thinking to himself, *It may not be long before King Moe, the despised despot, finds himself without anyone to command.*

Miles away, King Larry smiled as he pressed the volume increase button on his remote control as Ted Koppel continued his program. He was confident Ted would not find the same kind of unrest among his subjects.

Koppel began. "Our look at the lives of three kings and their kingdoms continues now as *Nightline* reporter Jeff Greenfield brings us this report from inside the kingdom of King Larry."

The king shifted uneasily in his bed as he saw Greenfield appear on the screen, walking down the main street of his kingdom. "King Larry rules in a mostly peaceful kingdom," the reporter began. A picture from 18 years earlier appeared on the screen, revealing a handsome young king assuming the throne. "When he was installed as king years ago, his subjects were thrilled. He was widely regarded as an intelligent, thoughtful and competent man who was well equipped to rule his subjects."

Greenfield continued. "And so he has ruled for the past 18 years. Today, however, the growing question in this kingdom is 'just exactly what does King Larry do?'"

King Larry winced as subjects in his kingdom began appearing on screen. "I guess he's a nice enough king," said one person, "and we've never lacked for basic services. We just don't seem to be going anywhere."

Two or three more subjects echoed similar thoughts before Greenfield introduced Professor Robert Weber Bly from the political science department at Kingdom State University. "King Larry's reign will be remembered as a somewhat unremarkable period in our history. He has successfully maintained steady economic growth, which seems to be where his main skills and interests lie. But he has shown little interest in domestic affairs, other than a desire to keep the peace. The times when his advisers have sought his counsel on some of the domestic issues facing the kingdom, they have been unable to engage him. His basic attitude seems to be, 'As long as I can keep the wheels of industry turning and can produce three percent growth in the GNP, then I'm doing my job.'"

Greenfield spoke again. "It appears, Ted, that this tiny kingdom is today being run more by frustrated advisers than it is by the king himself. And while King Larry gets high marks from his citizens for his economic programs, there is a growing sense in this kingdom that his subjects were really expecting something more from their ruler."

As Greenfield signed off, King Larry walked to his bathroom for a couple of Rolaids. He was doing his best, he told himself. He couldn't help it if domestic affairs intimidated him. It wasn't a science like economic affairs. He'd had no training in that area. Sure, his people were facing some serious domestic issues, and his chief adviser in that area was worried about his apparent lack of interest. It wasn't that he lacked interest, but he just had no idea what the answers were to most of the issues.

King Larry sighed. *Maybe*, he thought, *if he had the castle painted like his chief domestic adviser wanted, she'd be happy.* He looked on his laptop for the phone number of the royal painting service.

King Rocky I was prepared for the worst. *Nightline* hadn't cut King Moe or King Larry any slack, and there was no reason to expect he would fare any better. While he waited through the commercial break, King Rocky I began to list in his own mind the issues that would probably come up. Half-dozen financial blunders came to mind. His lack of experience in financial affairs had led to some economic hard times for his subjects early in his reign. There were also a handful of policy decisions he had made (over the objection of his trusted policy advisers) where he had been decisive—and clearly wrong. He had angered some of his subjects with those choices, and his approval ratings had dipped very low. On more than one occasion, he had gone on national television, admitted his mistakes and asked his people for forgiveness. He fully expected to see one of those embarrassing apologies replayed on TV during the next few minutes.

King Rocky I sat back in his bed. The economy in his kingdom was growing at a much slower rate than in King Larry's kingdom. The frustration some of his subjects expressed openly made him wonder at times if he should rule a little more like King Moe, where subjects did as they were commanded.

He had decided when he became king many years ago that he would not measure his performance against that of his contemporaries. Now here was Ted Koppel doing it for him. He thought about the danger of comparison as he pulled a book from his nightstand and opened its worn pages. The book told the story of the greatest King who had ever ruled in the region. King Rocky I had tried (unsuccessfully, he reminded himself) to pattern his reign after the reign of that long-ago King. He was sure his failures were about to be viewed by an audience of millions.

The commercials ended and the theme music began. "We turn now to another king and his kingdom," said Ted Koppel. "If you'll forgive the pun, it's a look inside a rocky reign . . ."

The Meaning of Kingship

Somewhere along the line, we got confused about what it means for a man to be a king.

Maybe we drew our conclusions about kingship from British royalty. We looked to England and assumed kingship meant power, privilege and position. We saw no real responsibilities other than the ceremonial, and a life where any material need is fulfilled on command. From American shores, a king's life has appeared to be the ultimate in selfish indulgence, with a few minor inconveniences cluttering up your existence.

In ancient times, the picture was very different. In spite of the warning of Yahweh, the nation of Israel insisted on being ruled by a king like the other Middle Eastern nations at that time. They were not looking for someone who would lead a privileged life in a castle somewhere. The Bible says the nation of Israel refused to listen to the warning of the prophet Samuel and said, "There shall be a king over us, that we also may be like all the nations, *that our king may judge us and go out before us and fight our battles*" (1 Sam. 8:19-20, emphasis added).

The kingly office then was defined in the eyes of the people as a position of responsibility and leadership, not of privilege and possessions. The king would be responsible to judge disputes, to lead the nation in peacetime and to serve as commander-in-chief of the armed forces. A king was charged with the divine duty of ruling with justice in the fear of God (see 2 Sam. 23:3). His ultimate responsibility was not to the people, since kings were not chosen by popular vote, but to the King of kings.

Author Dan Allender offers an enlightening job description for the kingly office. As you read his words, consider how a husband is called into kingly service to his wife:

The king led, protected and provided for the safety of the realm. He secured the infrastructure necessary for civilization. He justly applied the law of God to the government, commerce and care of the state. . . . The king was not only a warrior, but he also was the representative of the realm in conversations with the "world." He planned strategies, negotiated alliances, and applied the word of God to daily conflicts. . . . In so doing, he became the one who took the truth of God into the world and invited unbelievers to know and bow before the God of Israel.[1]

The husband-king is called to the same responsibilities. He leads his wife. He is her provider. He is her protector. He is the judge who knows and applies the law of God in the home. A husband is responsible to represent his wife and his family in society.

In His incarnation, Jesus was not only the perfect prophet of God and our great high priest, but He also was revealed as King of heaven and earth. He is once again our model for how we as husbands are to rule in our homes.

Loving Leadership

Much has been written in our day about the paradox of servant-leadership. When two of the disciples asked for positions of prestige in the coming Kingdom, Jesus explained a different plan:

> You know that the rulers of the Gentiles lord it over them, and their great men exercise authority over them. It is not this way among you, but whoever wishes to become great among you shall be your servant, and whoever wishes to be first among you shall be your slave; just as the Son of Man did not come to be served, but to serve, and to give His life a ransom for many (Matt. 20:25-28).

As pastor and author Robert Lewis points out masterfully in his book *Rockin' the Roles*, the husband's responsibility to be "head" of his wife does not give him the right to be a King Moe-style "lording" leader. Nor does it allow him the option of being a responsibility-shirking King

Larry—a "passive" leader. The divine design is for a husband to follow the rocky road of loving leadership in his marriage.

Because many men have abused their authority as husbands and as leaders, they have tended to emphasize their roles as servants. Slowly, men are shaking off the passive detachment that defined a generation of husbands. Men are beginning to assume their biblical responsibility to serve their wives, demonstrating their service through sacrificial action. But in the process of emphasizing service, men may have oversold their case. Unless that sacrificial love is expressed by bold, biblically ordered husbands who assume both leadership and responsibility for their homes, they will have simply traded one grievous error for another less obvious one. Many husbands have made service the *sine qua non* of husbandry, and in the process, have missed the point. When we talk about a husband who is a servant leader, "leader" is a noun and "servant," while also a noun, serves as a modifier. In other words, a husband is not to be a servant who serves by leading. He is called by God to be a leader, whose leadership is characterized by service.[2]

Like most husbands, I've been guilty throughout much of my married life of emphasizing service and shirking my responsibilities as a leader. In a desire to "serve" my wife and to avoid conflict, I have sometimes deferred to her desires or her preferences. On the surface, there is nothing wrong with that. I have sacrificially died to self in a desire to please her. In the process, though, I've assumed that my self-sacrifice and service pleased God.

Over time, the subtle message she has received has been that I will usually yield to her wishes or opinions. My "leadership" has sometimes been a puppet regime, where I lead by trying to do whatever my wife wanted me to do. That's a phony kind of leadership that says, "I'm in charge here, and I say we should do whatever you think is right!"

Men who serve without leading are ultimately doing their wives a great injustice. They *are* asking their wives to assume a responsibility God did not create them to bear. In Genesis 3, God announces the consequences of Adam's and Eve's disobedience:

To the woman He said, "I will greatly multiply your pain in childbirth, in pain you shall bring forth children; yet *your desire will be for your husband, and he will rule over you"* (v. 16, emphasis added).

There is general agreement among conservative commentators that the phrase "your desire will be for your husband" should be understood to mean that Eve would now seek to control or to rule over her husband.[3] Keil and Delitzsch call it a "desire bordering on a disease."[4] The accompanying phrase, "he will rule over you," sets up the tension that has existed in every husband and wife relationship since the Fall—the responsibility of the husband to rule and the desire of the wife ultimately to be in charge.

Essentially, the husband who "serves" his wife by continually yielding to her desires or her wishes is in fact asking her to do his job for him. He's ignoring his responsibility to lead.

As counter cultural as this will sound, God has designed marriage so that a woman is to be under the authority of her husband. It's not because she is inferior to her husband in her decision-making abilities. She is gifted by God in very special ways as a woman. She has been created with equal value and equal worth. We're not talking about ability or about value. We're talking about function. God's design is that a wife should look to her husband for leadership and direction for her life. She should want him to lead her and be ready to submit to his leadership as to Christ.

It follows, then, that those of us who are husbands have a divine responsibility to lead our wives. We must not demean our wives by failing to respect the abilities and gifts God has given them. In fact, we ought to view our wives as joint heirs of the grace of God and colaborers with Christ (see Rom. 8:17). If our family were a corporation, our wives would be the chief operating officer, working hand in hand with us as the chief executive officer. Equal in value yet different in function.

We are to help our wives employ their gifts and abilities in God's service. A husband is given the God-ordained task of helping his wife to be all that God intends for her to be.

A few years ago, my wife and I faced a difficult decision together. The church youth group was taking students on a mission trip to a Central

American country, and our 15-year-old daughter wanted to go. The trip appeared to be a well-supervised event, and many of Amy's friends were signed up.

As Mary Ann and I discussed the trip, it was obvious that she had concerns. Amy was young. She'd be a long way from decent medical care if anything should happen. Were we setting a precedent that younger brothers and sisters would point to later on? Even though she'd be going with her classmates, she'd still be one of the youngest children on the trip. Maybe we should wait a year.

I also talked with Amy about the trip. Why did she want to go? What about raising the funds? I explained some of our concerns, and she let me know that she would accept whatever decision her mom and I reached. (I found out later that her Bible-study group at church was praying that we would allow her to go. It's an interesting feeling to know you've got a group of high schoolers praying for you to exercise your parental authority in a certain way.)

This was one of those rare, difficult times when Mary Ann and I were split on our decision. Her concerns were entirely valid. I knew there were risks, but I also believed the experience would be positive for Amy. Mary Ann didn't disagree. She thought we ought to wait a year or two before we said yes.

I prayed for days. I sought the counsel of others. Mary Ann and I talked about the pros and cons of the trip. In the end, we agreed that the final decision was up to me.

One night before we had to say yes or no, I talked again with Mary Ann.

"There's one thing that keeps haunting me," I told her. "I think to myself, *If I decide to let Amy go and something does happen, will you hold me responsible?*" We talked that night about how hard it is to face a decision like this as a man, knowing that I bear the responsibility for what happens. Was she willing to "go along" with my decision, or did she really trust that God was directing and leading me, no matter what might happen?

In the end, I had to choose what seemed right to me for our family. In this case, it meant deciding that Amy could go. I knew that, in spite of our discussion, it would be humanly very difficult for Mary Ann not to hold me accountable if something did go wrong. It would be hard for her to trust any future decisions I would make.

As Amy boarded her plane for her week-long trip to Honduras, I prayed, "O Lord, keep her safe. For her sake. And for mine!" When she returned a week later, safe, sound and excited about her trip, I could see that God had given her a fresh understanding of what it means to follow Christ. It was an experience that would mark her life.

Did that mean my decision was right, or that Mary Ann's concerns were wrong? No. It simply meant that a decision had to be reached. Someone had to make the call. After prayer and counsel, I did what I thought was right at the time, and it turned out okay.

The fact that God gives men the responsibility to make the final decision in situations like this is no guarantee that we won't make some bad decisions. That's part of the price of leadership. The authority to lead and to make final decisions does not mean that a husband now has license to "get his way" so that his wife will learn to submit. We still have the responsibility as Christlike husbands to die to self! As a leader, though, we must lovingly guide and shepherd our wives in the way God would have them go, even if they resist our leadership.

The responsibility for a husband here is great! We must be actively seeking to know the will of God, not only for our own life, but also for our wife's life. When we lead, we must be careful to rule in the fear of God (see 2 Sam. 23:3). We have been given the responsibility to care for the spiritual, emotional, physical and social needs of our wife. Our authority and leadership should never be focused on any benefit we might receive in the process. We are to use our authority to glorify God, to advance the work of His Kingdom and to lead our wife in growing in grace and Christlikeness.

Helpful Hints for a Servant-King

The last line of the movie *My Fair Lady* is stunning in its chauvinism. I watched the video again a few years ago, singing along merrily with "The Rain in Spain" and "I Could Have Danced All Night." I was caught up in the charm and romance, unprepared for the cultural shock I was about to receive.

As the movie ends, the confirmed bachelor Henry Higgins is beginning to realize that he may have romantic feelings for his student, the recently transformed Eliza Doolittle. After having treated her shabbily, he now misses her and longs for her to return. She, on the other hand, has been the object of his snobbish scorn throughout the movie. She has been little more than a linguistics experiment for him. Still, the professor has somehow captured her heart, and she finds herself drawn to him.

She creeps into his den, where he is lost in his melancholy, singing about the young woman to whom he has grown accustomed. Without seeing her, he somehow senses her presence in the room.

Does he turn to her, begging forgiveness for the way he has mistreated and abused her? Does he drop his head in shame and beg her to return to him?

No. Without missing a beat, he smiles a sly smile and says, "Eliza, where the devil are my slippers?" She runs to embrace him, the music swells and the credits roll.

Got it? He tells her (in so many words) to fetch his slippers and the two are reunited in their love. One can only imagine that if the movie were made today and Higgins were to deliver the same closing, Eliza would kick Henry in the stomach and run to the arms of the properly domesticated Freddy Eynsford-Hill.

But a generation ago no one apparently thought twice about the right of a man to be the King Moe of his castle. By the way, when you're done fetching the slippers, bring me the pipe and keep the children quiet while I read the paper.

Most of us as men have seen the kingly office abused so often by now that we don't have a good picture of how a king is supposed to fulfill his duties. We have accepted the "lording leader" as a distorted view of authority. After years of living as passive King Larrys, we have come to regard passivity as sin and begun what one speaker calls "the quest for authentic manhood."[5]

For the sake of our wives, we must once again assume our true kingly roles as leaders who execute our leadership with humble hearts and loving service for our wives. Here are some practical steps we as husbands can take as we seek to take on the mantle of a servant-king.

Examine Your Leadership

Are you a King Moe or a King Larry? Are you a dictator or a do-nothing kind of guy? Have you taken on the responsibility of serving your wife but ignored the task of leading her?

You're in there somewhere. Almost certainly, you have a natural, sinful pattern that characterizes your leadership. When you slip up as a husband, you probably find yourself slipping in the same direction over and over again.

God wants to steady your footing. You must begin by agreeing with Him that you have a tendency to be a lording leader, a passive leader or a husband who serves instead of leading.

Failing to live up to God's standard in any area is what the Bible refers to as sin. When we agree with God that our actions fall short of His established design, we are confessing our sins to Him.

But it doesn't end there. Confession is the beginning, not the end. We must not only turn away from sin, but we also must turn toward Christ. God is calling us to repent, to change. We are to lock our sights on the example of the perfect leader and then follow in His footsteps. As we grow in our understanding of our role as husband-king, and as we begin to apply the truth of Scripture in our marriage, God will make us into the kind of leaders He has called us to become.

Start Leading

I have never forgotten what C. S. Lewis wrote in *Mere Christianity* about how we acquire virtues. "Very often," he said, "the only way to get a quality is to start behaving as if you had it already."

As husband and wife, it's time to sit down and begin to discuss areas in your marriage where you need to start showing some leadership. Ask your wife to point out for you areas where you can be leading her and your family. It may be something as simple as initiating daily prayer with your wife. It may involve setting up a savings account to plan for future needs and then making regular deposits. Examine the major areas of your family and your life: your faith, your marriage, your children, your job, your relationships with friends, your service to the community, your physical health and well-being, your stewardship over the resources God has given you and your recreational time. Then decide where you need to begin to take some initiative and lead.

As you lead, make sure to check your heart. Are you making decisions that you believe will bring honor and glory to Christ and that will lead both you and your wife to grow in your relationship with Him? How do you stand to gain from the decisions you're making? Remember, when you exercise your leadership for selfish purposes, you're abusing the important responsibility God has given you.

Learn to Judge in Righteousness

I've already made reference twice in this chapter to 2 Samuel 23:3-4. That passage is the dying advice King David gives to his son Solomon on how he is to lead God's people:

> The God of Israel said, the Rock of Israel spoke to me, "He who rules over men righteously, who rules in the fear of God, is as the light of the morning when the sun rises, a morning without clouds, when the tender grass springs out of the earth, through sunshine after rain."

If your leadership in the home is characterized by righteousness and by the fear of God, it will be like a beautiful spring morning to all who live in your home. That makes it incumbent on you as a husband to be a disciplined student of God's Word, so that you might exercise your authority in wisdom. To the extent that you lean on your own wisdom and understanding as the source of your authority, you will be abusing your kingly office.

Again, it's no wonder why our culture has given up on the concept of men leading and ruling in their homes. Not only have men used their authority for selfish gain, but they have failed to rule in the wisdom and counsel of God. It's easy to understand why women have judged male leadership at home as a failure and have looked for a way to reinterpret the command of Scripture.

Even in a position of authority, a husband is not the ultimate authority. That distinction belongs to God and to His Word. Husbands must look to Him for direction and guidance on how they are to lead their wives.

Do Some Strategic Planning

In his books *Tender Warrior* and *The Four Pillars of a Man's Heart*, pastor and author Stu Weber expands our thinking on the husband's role as "provider." The root word, Weber explains, means to "see ahead" ("pro"—ahead or before, and "vision"—to see). A provider does much more than to secure material necessities. He makes strategic plans for his marriage and his home, looking ahead to arrange for spiritual, emotional and social needs as well.

Most successful businesses have a strategic plan, mapping out where the company is headed over the next 5 to 10 years. Things change, of course, and the businesses adapt. But they work hard to consider market conditions, examine competing organizations, assess their own strengths and weaknesses, look for opportunities on the horizon and then set the course for their business.

Many of those same businessmen, who can establish a successful plan for a company, are clueless when it comes time to think strategically about the spiritual, emotional, physical and social needs of their wives. Ask them about their five-year plan for their marriage, and you're likely to get a deer-in-the-headlights look.

In their book, *Intimate Allies*, authors Dan Allender and Tremper Longman III write about this aspect of how a husband should function as king in marriage:

> We are called to cultivate Christ in our spouses. . . . To do so effectively, we must be guided by a vision of who they are, a picture of who they were meant to be (like Christ) and a grasp of our role in helping them become like Christ.[6]

Later, during a *FamilyLife Today* radio interview about the book, Allender talked about spending time writing a short-term mission statement for his wife. When he began explaining the idea, I thought it sounded presumptuous. But as Dan talked about encouraging and exhorting his wife to become all God wants her to be as a woman, as a wife and as a mother, it was clear he was not being presumptuous. He was being the kind of kingly husband his wife ultimately wants and needs him to be.

Gentlemen, it's up to us. God has put us in charge. Have we prayerfully sought to map out a plan for the next five years of our marriage? It's time for some pro-vision. It's time to look ahead and make some plans.

Stay Alert

Resistance to your assuming leadership in your marriage will come from all directions. It will come from a culture that is increasingly drifting farther away from God's standards and is pulling your marriage along in its undertow. It will come from friends and coworkers who thinking themselves to be wise have become as fools (see Rom. 1:22).

It will come from some surprising places. Today there are many evangelical churches that have lost their confessional moorings and their confidence in the absolute standards of God's Word. It shouldn't surprise you to hear popular ideas about a husband's role in marriage coming from books, radio, television and even from church pulpits that aren't rooted in biblical truth. A wise husband will test everything he reads or hears—even this book—against the absolute standard of the Bible.

There will also be resistance from your closest ally—your wife. While her spirit will welcome the leadership, protection and provision of a wise king, her flesh will war against her spirit and will seek to thwart your authority. Over time, there will probably be showdowns, as you wrestle with whether to compromise and gain her approval or to stand fast and make her angry! There will be times when you'll have to decide whether to serve her or to serve God.

Perhaps the greatest source of resistance as you seek to be faithful to God's calling as a husband will come from your own flesh. You will slip into patterns and habits that come from years of living in rebellion to the things of God. You'll lack the confidence to lead. You'll lack the desire to serve. You'll look around and think, *I'm doing better than most husbands*, and you'll settle for less than God's best.

The apostle Paul knew that the issue of authority and submission was a spiritual minefield. It is in that specific context that he warns all Christians to "be strong in the Lord and in the strength of His might. Put on the full armor of God, so that you will be able to stand firm against the schemes of the devil" (Eph. 6:10-11). God has made provision for you to be able to stand strong in the face of opposition to His plan.

In her prayer of dedication for her son, Hannah said, "Those who contend with the LORD will be shattered; against them He will thunder in the heavens, the LORD will judge the ends of the earth; and He will give strength to His king, and will exalt the horn of His anointed" (1 Sam. 2:10). The enemy may trip you up, but in the strength of the Lord you will not be defeated.

The Old Testament records for us the multiplied failures of the kings of Israel and Judah. Dan Allender comments on how few honored their unique calling:

> Far too often the kings compromised truth in making alliances that violated God's desire. They allowed for worship of the false gods associated with the nations with which they had formed alliances. This led to grave injustice, perversion, and a loss of freedom and safety. This perversion of power was seldom condemned in the cultus, but it was roundly exposed by the prophetic community. Eventually, God cleansed the subversion of his rule by sending his people into exile.[7]

We must be husbands who follow the calling and example not of the Old Testament monarchs, but of the King of kings. He has called us out of darkness and into the Kingdom of light. He is at work in us, conforming us to His image. He does not rescue us from every trial, but He sends us through them that we might grow. He is the servant King who willingly lays down His life for His sheep, but who calls us to take up our Cross and to follow Him. Sometimes He leads us beside still waters; other times He points us toward the valley of the shadow of death (see Ps. 23). We can resist, but we soon learn that it is better to obey than to kick against the goad.

In Closing

As husbands, we have been assigned the kingly task of leading our wives on our pilgrimage through earth to heaven. We serve her not when we do everything she asks us to do, but when we understand and cooperate with the sanctifying work of the Holy Spirit in her life. We never see our kingly office as an opportunity for privilege, but as a divine responsibility to lead her as she grows in grace.

PointstoConsider

1. When you hear the word "king," what picture comes to your mind?
2. What do 1 Samuel 8:19-20 and 23:2-4 say about the role and responsibilities of a king?
3. How would you apply these concepts to a man's responsibilities as "king" in his home?
4. A husband is called to be a "servant leader" in his home. According to the chapter, "He is called by God to be a leader, whose leadership is characterized by service." In what ways do you need to begin serving your wife? In what ways do you need to begin leading her?
5. What happens in a home when a husband ignores his responsibility to lead?

PART THREE

THE
TASK:HOWTO
REALLYLOVEYOUR
WIFE

"**C**ongratulations, Mr. Lepine. Based on our initial interviews, we are now ready to consider you as a candidate for the position of husband."

"Thank you. Can I be honest?"

"Of course."

"I wasn't sure I was going to make it this far. I had no idea there was so much involved in being a husband!"

"Most men don't, Mr. Lepine. And their performance reflects that lack of understanding."

"That stuff about being a prophet, a priest and a king to my wife was all new to me."

"Now that you understand what the position involves, do you feel you can carry out the duties?"

"Honestly? I don't know. I've never done anything like this before. But I am a fast learner, and I promise to work very hard. I really want the position."

"That is all evident in how you've responded in the interviews so far. In fact, that's why you're still in the running. We have eliminated some better-qualified candidates who don't appear to have the same desire you have. We have learned to expect some level of failure in all successful candidates. We gave up looking for a 'perfect' applicant a long time ago. We want applicants who can admit their failures and move forward."

"So what now?"

"This is the final phase of our process. You have demonstrated an understanding of the necessary qualifications and of the basic responsibilities associated with the position. Now we focus on the job description—the actual work you'll be doing each day."

"Like bringing home the groceries and mowing the lawn?"

"Like loving your wife."

"Is that it? That's easy. I already love her."

"I'm not talking about how you *feel* about her. I'm talking about the hard work of loving a wife and doing it well."

"But I'm already good at this! Really! Ask Mary Ann."

"I'm not so sure . . ."

"Last week, I sent her three cards that said 'thinking of you.' I brought her daisies. I figured anyone can do roses. I wanted to be creative, so I brought her daisies."

"Mr. Lepine . . ."

"Have you talked to her? Did she tell you about the Valentine's Day when I got the pizza guy to make a heart-shaped pizza and took it to where she was working? Or the shirt I had made for her with her pet name, 'Honey Bunny,' sewn on it?"

"Mr. Lepine . . ."

"The point here is that I already love her. That's why I want to marry her. I'm going to have no problem on this part."

"I'm afraid this part has very little to do with heart-shaped pizzas."

"Huh?"

"Romance and passion are a part of what makes a marriage work. But that's not what we're focusing on here. We're talking about loving your wife."

"I know, that's what . . ."

" . . . as Christ loved the Church. Remember?"

"Oh. Yeah."

"There were no 'thinking of you' notes involved."

"I guess not. So, are you telling me all that mushy stuff counts for nothing?"

"That 'mushy stuff,' as you call it, counts. But it's not the essence of what it means really to love your wife well."

"Okay, so what do I need to know? I'm not giving up on this."

"You'd better give up."

"Huh?"

"That's what the Bible says in Ephesians 5:25: 'Husbands, love your wives, just as Christ also loved the church and gave Himself up for her.'"

"So, you're talking about the 'dying to self' stuff?"

"Yes. But it's more than that. The day-to-day work of being a husband also involves being an agent of sanctification."

"This is beginning to sound like a lot of work."

"It is. You're also responsible to nourish and cherish your wife."

"You mean 'nourish' as in 'feed'?"

"Not exactly. You'd better get comfortable. It looks as if we're going to be here for a while."

CHAPTER 9

LOVE HER WITH COMMITMENT

The first time I told Mary Ann that I loved her was a few weeks after we had started dating. What a mistake! I was completely unaware of all that those three words communicate to a young woman. I had no idea what I was really saying to her. What I meant was, "You're nice and I like spending time with you." What she heard was, "I'm fully and exclusively committed to you."

My watered-down, mediocre definition of love was a reflection of the spirit of the age. We live in an era when the greatness of what it means to love another person has been diluted to its lowest common denominator. When we talk about a "great lover," we usually mean someone who expresses passion during sex. We talk casually about loving everything from golf to a particular brand of hot dogs and, in the process, our understanding of what real love is has been cheapened beyond recognition.

In the classic Ephesians 5 passage on a husband's responsibility in marriage, the apostle Paul writes that husbands are to love their wives "just as Christ also loved the church" (v. 25). Paul goes on to explain that the dominant characteristic of that love was His sacrifice, giving up His life for us. The apostle John explains it this way:

> We know love by this, that He laid down His life for us; and we ought to lay down our lives for the brethren (1 John 3:16).

Most husbands will never be called upon to physically suffer and die for their wives. The death of Christ on the cross may be the ultimate expression of His love for us, but it is not the exclusive expression of His love. To become a "great lover" in the biblical sense of the expression, we must examine four very specific ways in which Christ has expressed His love for His Church.

Unconditional Love

Somewhere back at the edge of eternity, before the heavens and the earth had been created, in the council of the Godhead, a divine plan was set in motion. Early in his letter to the Church at Ephesus, Paul described the plan this way:

> He chose us in Him before the foundation of the world, that we would be holy and blameless before Him. In love He predestined us to adoption as sons through Jesus Christ to Himself, according to the kind intention of His will, to the praise of the glory of His grace, which He freely bestowed on us in the Beloved (Eph. 1:4-6).

Long before we were knit together in our mothers' wombs, when all we were was an idea in the mind of God, the Bible teaches that God loved us. Having set apart His people from among every tongue and tribe on Earth, God's first act of love toward His new Bride was to establish our destiny, choosing to adopt us as His own children. He knew we would be a rebellious, disobedient lot, and He made provision for our rebellion in Christ.

Why did He choose to love us, long before He created us? Some of us get confused at this point, thinking that God's holy, transcendent love is like our love for one another. For us, the first step toward a loving relationship with another person begins with some kind of attraction. A man is usually first drawn to a particular woman in the same way Samson was drawn to his Philistine wife:

> Then Samson went down to Timnah and saw a woman in Timnah, one of the daughters of the Philistines. So he came back and told his father and mother, "I saw a woman in Timnah, one of the daughters of the Philistines; now therefore, get her for me as a wife." Then his father and his mother said to him, "Is there no woman among the daughters of your relatives, or among all our people, that you go to take a wife from the uncircumcised Philistines?" But Samson said to his father, "Get her for me, for *she looks good to me*" (Judg. 14:1-3, emphasis added).

A man is drawn into a relationship with a woman usually because of her beauty or her charm, which, according to the Proverbs, is vain and deceitful (see 31:30). Not so with God. His love for us has nothing to do with how attractive we are, either physically (after all, He is the One who creates us) or spiritually (in our sin, we were spiritually dead). His love for us is not based in any way on how we will perform. He does not find us attractive because, as some have suggested, He looks down the corridors of time and is drawn to those who would one day choose to follow Him.

No. According to Scripture, there is only one reason why God chose us to be His adopted sons. It is because it was "the kind intention of His will, to the praise of the glory of His grace" (Eph. 1:5-6). To put it another way, God chose us as His adopted sons because He wanted to—pure and simple. By choosing us, He was able to put on display the glory of His grace for all the world to see.

Thus, the first way in which Christ demonstrated His love for His Church was by choosing us to be the recipients of His mercy and His grace. His decision had nothing to do with our worthiness to be the objects of His love. He didn't wait to love the lovable. He chose to love us because it pleased Him to do so.

If a husband is to love his wife "as Christ also loved the church" (Eph. 5:25), he must begin by loving her with the same kind of unconditional acceptance Christ demonstrated in choosing to love us. Husbands must love their wives, not based on subjective factors like appearance or performance, but because they choose to love their wives no matter what.

One husband in the Bible provides for us a portrait of a man choosing to love even an unlovable wife. His name was Hosea, and God called him to be a prophet. Most prophets were set apart by God to announce the word of the Lord to the people of God (who usually weren't interested in hearing it). Hosea had a different assignment. God called him to provide the nation of Israel with a living example of God's love for them.

One day the word of the Lord came to Hosea. God said, "Go, take to yourself a wife of harlotry and have children of harlotry; for the land commits flagrant harlotry, forsaking the LORD" (Hos. 1:2).

Imagine. As a prophet, Hosea had been called by God and set apart for divine service. One morning, he awakens to hear the voice of God—his marching orders. He has waited to hear from God how he might be used to bring honor to his creator.

"Your assignment," God tells Hosea, "is to marry a woman who will be unfaithful to you. She will abandon you and your children and will become a prostitute. She will bring you great shame. While your marriage bed lies empty, she will be giving herself willingly to any man who will pay her for her services.

"Her harlotry will lead her to slavery. She will be sold into slavery to satisfy the debts she accumulates. She will be taken to the slave auction, where she will be stripped naked and sold as a slave to the highest bidder. When this happens, you are to buy her back and again make her your wife."

Hosea was about to become a living parable. God's prophetic assignment was for Hosea to proclaim and demonstrate through his marriage God's unconditional love for His chosen Bride.

Hosea's faithfulness to God's call is even more remarkable when considered in the context of the culture in Hosea's day. A husband had the right, according to the custom of the day, to divorce his wife for any cause. If she failed to please him for any reason, he was permitted to march around her saying, "I divorce you" three times, and the act was complete. He was free to find another wife who would please him. At the same time, the punishment for marital unfaithfulness, according to the law, was death by stoning. Not only did Hosea have the right to divorce Gomer for her unfaithfulness, but she deserved to be put to death.

God's command for Hosea was that he love his wife in spite of her unfaithfulness. He was to choose to love her even though she had abandoned him. He was to be a living illustration of mercy, not justice. She would not receive what she deserved. She would receive instead the love of a husband that she apparently didn't want or deserve. To add insult to injury, Hosea would humble himself in the middle of the marketplace and pay good money to buy back the bride who had left him to become a prostitute.

The life of Hosea is a living illustration of the unconditional love of God, who chooses to love us, not because we have earned or deserved His love, but because it pleases Him to love us.

Surgeon Dr. Richard Selzer caught a glimpse of unconditional love after he performed a procedure on a young woman that left her face disfigured. How would her young husband react when he saw her? Selzer recalls:

> I stand by the bed where a young woman lies, her face postoperative, her mouth twisted in palsy, clownish. A tiny twig of the facial nerve, the one to the muscles of her mouth, has been severed. The surgeon had followed with religious fervor the curve of her flesh; I promise you that. Nevertheless, to remove the tumor in her cheek, I had cut the little nerve.
>
> Her young husband is in the room. He stands on the opposite side of the bed, and together they seem to dwell in the evening lamplight, isolated from me, private. *Who are they,* I ask myself, *he and this wrymouth I have made, who gaze at and touch each other so generously, greedily?* The young woman speaks.
>
> "Will my mouth always be like this?" she asks.
>
> "Yes," I say, "it will. It is because the nerve was cut."

She nods, and is silent. But the young man smiles.

"I like it," he says. "It is kind of cute."

All at once I know who he is. I understand, and I lower my gaze. One is not bold in an encounter with a god. Unmindful, he bends to kiss her crooked mouth, and I am so close I can see how he twists his own lips to accommodate to hers, to show her that their kiss still works.[1]

That's what unconditional love looks like. It's a "no matter what" kind of love. A husband who would love his wife as Christ also has loved the Church will begin by understanding that his love is a choice, made in spite of (not because of) his wife's actions, attitudes and appearance. Once he has called her to be his wife, a husband makes a pledge of unconditional love for his wife, for better or worse.

Covenantal Love

A husband loves his wife by making a covenant with her and keeping it, no matter what. He is a covenant keeper.

A Pledge

What was decided in eternity past—God's unconditional love for His Bride—was then established and declared by God in a series of covenants. Having chosen us in Him before the foundation of the world, God announced His intent, pledging to us that He will fulfill what He has purposed to do.

On a cloudless night in the Middle Eastern desert, God made a three-part promise to Abraham: (1) he would possess the land that God had given him; (2) he would have an heir; and (3) his descendants would number more than the stars in the sky. According to the Scriptures, Abraham believed the promise of God, and it was reckoned to him as righteousness. Even though he believed God, Abraham still asked God for some assurance. "He said, 'O Lord God, how may I know that I will possess it?'" (Gen. 15:8).

God did not rebuke Abraham for his question. Instead, He used a ceremony common in the ancient world to seal the pledge in blood:

So He said to him, "Bring Me a three year old heifer, and a three year old female goat, and a three year old ram, and a turtledove, and a young pigeon." Then he brought all these to Him and cut them in two, and laid each half opposite the other; but he did not cut the birds.

Now when the sun was going down, a deep sleep fell upon Abram; and behold, terror and great darkness fell upon him. God said to Abram, "Know for certain that your descendants will be strangers in a land that is not theirs, where they will be enslaved and oppressed four hundred years. But I will also judge the nation whom they will serve, and afterward they will come out with many possessions. And as for you, you shall go to your fathers in peace; you will be buried at a good old age. Then in the fourth generation they will return here, for the iniquity of the Amorite is not yet complete."

It came about when the sun had set, that it was very dark, and behold, there appeared a smoking oven and a flaming torch which passed between these pieces. On that day the LORD made a covenant with Abram, saying, "To your descendants I have given this land, from the river of Egypt as far as the great river, the river Euphrates: the Kenite and the Kenizzite and the Kadmonite and the Hittite and the Perizzite and the Rephaim and the Amorite and the Canaanite and the Girgashite and the Jebusite" (vv. 9-10,12-21).

Why, one might ask, did God answer Abraham's question with a covenant?

Let me suggest four reasons. First, God was inviting all generations to inspect His character. He had declared His plan and had performed the ancient equivalent of having a sworn statement notarized.

Second, in His covenant with Abraham, God revealed more specifics about His plan. By announcing to Abraham details of Israel's slavery in

Egypt and of the Exodus, God offered tangible evidence for future gen erations that His word can be trusted.

Third, God's relationship with Abraham was now defined on the basis of His covenant. Of all the people on the earth, God had selected Abraham to be the one with whom He would have a covenant relationship.

Finally, the covenant made it clear that God's faithfulness was not based on human response. This was not a contract where if one person reneges, the other is free. By passing between the animal carcasses, God was saying, "I'll do what I promise, no matter what. Count on it."

On his wedding day, a man takes his unconditional love for a woman and marks it in a covenantal ceremony. He stands before God and witnesses and takes a vow to love, honor and cherish his wife, in sickness and in health, for richer, for poorer, for better or for worse, *for as long as they both shall live.*

Although the modern wedding ceremony does not include a stroll between the split carcasses of wild animals (try suggesting that to your wedding planner), the pledge is just as binding. Our covenant is one more way that our marriage is designed to mirror the relationship between Christ and His Church.

This is no trivial matter. In the same way that God invites us to see His character on display in His faithfulness to keep His covenant with Abraham, so a man stakes his personal integrity on his faithfulness to his wedding vow. This is no longer the case in our culture, where divorce is all too common. The erosion of faithfulness to the marriage covenant in society has led us to a general disregard for issues of honesty and integrity. We vote for politicians who promise to lower taxes, even though we don't really believe they'll do it. We sign contracts and then run to a lawyer to find the loophole when we no longer want to honor the agreement.

A man who vows to love and care for his wife throughout his lifetime, no matter what, is inviting his community to examine his character. When he later tires of the relationship or violates his vow to it through infidelity, he expects that his "private" life should have no bearing on his "public" integrity. And our culture buys it. We no longer see a failure to honor a marriage vow as a serious flaw in a man's character, both public and private. We invent phrases like "his marriage failed" to attempt to disguise his personal role in its dissolution.

A vow taken before a holy God is nothing with which to trifle:

> When you make a vow to God, do not be late in paying it; for He takes no delight in fools. Pay what you vow! It is better that you should not vow than that you should vow and not pay (Eccles. 5:4-5).

If that's true in money matters, how much more true is it for a wedding vow?

The wedding vow is also a specific pledge a husband makes with his wife. We have come to think of the words spoken by a husband to a wife as some poetic or romantic phrases stuck together that work like a magic incantation—you say them and, poof, you're married! Nobody really pays any attention to the words themselves. Like other ritual language we mindlessly recite in church, the wedding vow is some nice-sounding, appropriately sober phrase that we mumble at the altar and immediately forget.

God did not inspire the specific words used in the vow. They are meant as a promise to fulfill the biblical mandate to love, honor and cherish a wife in any circumstance that comes along. It is not simply a promise to remain married. Imagine a contemporary wedding ceremony where a groom faces his bride and repeats the preacher's words: "I, Paul, promise not to get a divorce from you!"

No, in the same way that God's covenant with Abraham was a promise to fulfill specific events in the future, our wedding vow is a pledge to execute the specific responsibilities of a husband as God has set them forth in Scripture.

A Reinforced Relationship

Our marriage covenant also changes the nature of our relationship. Most of us men can remember some of the awkward ambiguity about our relationship that existed before we were engaged. At some point, one of us initiated a delicate conversation with the other, wanting to give some definition to it all. We asked questions such as "Where is this thing headed?" or "Do you like me the same way I'm starting to like you?"

In the latter half of the twentieth century, those conversations have often been followed by a mutual decision to take the plunge and move in together. In addition to pragmatic considerations, most couples who live together before marriage think of it as a step up from a serious dating relationship, where many of the benefits of marriage are enjoyed without the pesky commitment to each other (beyond, that is, the commitment of the moment).

This postadolescent "pretending to be married without the binding obligations of a marriage license" fails to live up to any of its promises. In 1998, the U.S. Census Bureau estimated that the number of unmarried couples living together has topped 4 million. According to an editorial in the *Indianapolis News*, a national study conducted over a 10-year period found that couples who live together before marriage are almost 35 percent more likely to get a divorce than couples who wait to move in until after the wedding. For couples who live together, get married and wind up staying together, studies show a higher rate of marital dissatisfaction. The newspaper concluded:

> There may be couples who enjoy healthy, lasting marriages following cohabitation, but this does not contradict the reality that it is an unwise move for couples to live together outside of marriage.[2]

At the same time, if couples live together and split up prior to ever tying the knot, they are left with devastating emotional baggage from that relationship. (Ask any therapist working today about his or her clients.) And studies show that those who continue living together outside of marriage reportedly engage in sexual relations less often than married couples. Presumably, that's one of the reasons they're living together, and even that's not working out!

A covenant changes things. It makes a man into a husband who is now committed and responsible for his wife throughout their life together. Instead of introducing your partner as "my friend," "my roommate" or "my significant other," we become man and wife.

The marriage covenant also reinforces our choice to unconditionally love another person. God's covenant with us is unconditional. His faithfulness is not based on our performance or any other circumstances. He doesn't fall out of love with us. His pledge that He will never leave us or forsake us is a promise we can take to the bank.

In the same way, our covenant with each other ought to press us back toward one another, even when the realities of the relationship are pushing us in the other direction. There was a reason our wedding vow talked about better or worse, sickness and health, and poverty and riches. We will all face days when the one to whom we are unconditionally committed is not particularly attractive. In that moment, we must love our mate with a covenantal love, just as we vowed we would do when we said "I do."

Incarnational Love

A few summers ago, I sat watching the Colorado Rockies play the Los Angeles Dodgers at Coors Field. I had been invited to join a group of friends at the ballpark, and our host was the president of a growing national company. Together that night, we watched the game from one of the plush skyboxes in the stadium.

Now, I grew up in St. Louis watching the Cardinals from the cheap seats at Busch Stadium (back in the days when there *were* cheap seats). I would go with a group of guys, and we'd sit two decks up, way down the right-field line. After a few innings, if the crowd was thin, we'd wander down a deck and try to find some better seats. The first deck was about as good as we could ever get. The ushers stood guard at the entrance to the box seats.

Watching a baseball game from a skybox was a new experience for me. Our seats were right behind third base. We had our food wheeled in on a silver cart. There were hot dogs for the traditionalists, along with an assortment of other items to munch on. We had a couple of TVs for instant replays. Had the weather been cool, we could have watched the game from behind the huge picture window. But since it was a nice evening, we sat out on the terrace. It was a great way to watch a ballgame. (The Rockies won, I think.)

Now imagine for a minute that you own your own skybox at the local stadium. In fact, imagine you are the co-owner of the stadium and the team! You travel to your box on a private elevator, your food is brought on silver carts and a team of waiters are just outside the door in case you need anything during the game. You have the best seats in the house at your disposal.

Let's say that you get a call one day from your partner. He has a plan that would require you to spend some time out of the skybox. You'll still get to see every game, but he'd like you to trade your interest in the sky-box for a single season ticket in the second to last row of the bleachers. You'll be sitting right in the middle of the beer and peanuts crowd, buying cold hot dogs and watered-down Cokes at high prices from the stadium vendors. You can expect to get beer sloshed down your back, to hear some pretty rough language and to be right in the middle of a few fights that break out.

To top it all off, you won't fit in with the crowd, and they'll know it. There will be a few fans who recognize you as a co-owner of the team, but most of the crowd will figure the owner would never sit in the bleachers. When the team goes through a losing season, they'll mock you and say, "I thought you were the owner. Can't you do anything about this?"

From the skybox to the bleachers—any takers?

Not likely.

Stepping into Her World

However unlikely it is, that choice to move from the penthouse to the cellar represents in a small way the second demonstration of divine love. The apostle John writes, "By this the love of God was manifested in us, that *God has sent His only begotten Son into the world* so that we might live through Him" (1 John 4:9, emphasis added). After adopting us as His children and pouring out His unconditional love on us, and after binding Himself to love us by a covenant, God moved to execute His plan. He stepped away from the throne room of heaven—the place of power and prerogative—and stepped onto a fallen planet, clothed in human flesh.

In Paul's letter to the Philippians, he explains that Jesus, "although He existed in the form of God, did not regard equality with God a thing to be grasped, but emptied Himself, taking the form of a bond-servant, and being made in the likeness of men" (Phil. 2:6-7).

From eternity past, the Son of God had lived where He deserved to live, with angels, cherubim and seraphim hovering around Him, praising His greatness and attending to any request. Because of His love for His Bride, He chose to step out of the palace and into the middle of a dung heap, knowing He would be despised and rejected by the same people to whom He had given the gift of life. To become the high priest who can sympathize with our weaknesses, and who has been tempted in all things as we are, yet without sin (see Heb. 4:15), He willingly laid aside His right to reign and rule, and became a bond servant instead.

A husband who seeks to love his wife in the same way that Christ loved His Church will not only love unconditionally and establish his relationship with a covenant, but he also will love incarnationally. His love for his wife will be characterized by setting aside any claim to privilege or prerogative and stepping into her world, learning to sympathize with her weaknesses.

Setting Aside His Own Desires

Incarnational love does not mean that a man trades in his masculinity for femininity. Pop psychology has had a lot to say in recent years about a man's feminine side. Marriage books everywhere today seem to suggest that for a marriage to work, a husband needs to become more relational, more communicative, more nurturing and more sensitive. In fact, some books that attempt to define real manhood seem to suggest that a real man is someone who learns how to act more like a woman when he is with his wife!

Make no mistake. In His incarnation, Jesus became "fully man." He was as much a human as you and I are. His single distinguishing characteristic that separated His humanity from ours is that He never sinned. His life as a man was in perfect submission to the will of God.

Thus, a husband who learns to love incarnationally will become a man who, like Jesus, learns to sympathize with the challenges his wife endures. He will willingly set aside any privilege he may think is associated with being her husband, like the right to watch *Monday Night Football* or to play 18 holes of golf on Saturday. He will embrace her life and her world as his own, loving her by choosing to live his life alongside her in all that she faces.

Before He sacrificed His life for us on the cross, Jesus had already laid aside His divine rights. Loving unconditionally will mean that we give up our own desires. It means that we arrive home from work in the evening not to be served and to relax, but to help get the kids ready for bed, to dry the dishes, to help fold laundry, to spend time talking about our day, to go to the grocery store, to help plan menus, to pay the bills, to empty the trash, to sit down with the family calendar and do some planning, and to listen to our wife's frustrations about the kids or her job or the other ladies in the Bible study. It means praying with our wife instead of watching Jay Leno. It means ignoring the mail and the newspaper until we have connected with her. It means setting aside the things we'd like to do and making it our priority to become part of her world.

One evening Mary Ann and I were attending a small group Bible study with other couples. We were using the HomeBuilders material that has been created by FamilyLife for couples to study together. At one point in the evening, each wife was to answer the question: What is the most romantic thing your mate has done recently?

Like every husband in the room, I began to wonder what my wife would share. I wondered if Mary Ann would tell about the cookies I had sent during a recent business trip. Would she tell about our tenth anniversary, when I surprised her with an out-of-town trip? Which of my romantic exploits would she divulge to the group?

When it was her turn, Mary Ann said, "The other night, I was in doing the dishes and Bob was watching TV. All of a sudden, without my saying anything, he turned off the TV, came into the kitchen and started drying dishes."

Huh?

That was romantic?

I realized later that the simple act of dish drying without having been asked to help was a statement of incarnational love. I had set aside my own comfort and had stepped into her world.

Let me suggest one additional example of incarnational love. Not long after our two daughters were born, we learned that we were going to be parents again. We had never made any conscious decision about the size of our family, and we were always excited when we found out that Mary Ann was pregnant. In fact, I was the one who wanted to get on the phone right away and start calling the relatives to share the good news. Mary Ann always preferred to wait awhile before we told anyone.

With this pregnancy, I learned at least one reason for her caution. She was still in the first trimester when she began to bleed. She went to bed immediately, taking every precaution to attempt to protect the little life inside her. But the bleeding didn't stop. What had become painfully obvious to us was confirmed a few days later by the doctor: Mary Ann had miscarried. She was no longer pregnant.

As a man, I will never know what it must be like to conceive and carry a child in your womb. I have seen the glow that radiates from the face of a woman who has found out she will be a mother again. During each of her pregnancies, I watched my wife go into what I jokingly referred to as "pregnancy mode." Almost overnight, she would adopt more cautious eating habits, begin a new routine of exercises and add vitamins to her diet. The baby inside her might not be as big as a fingernail yet, but there was already a bond beginning to form between mother and child.

So when a wife gets news that she has miscarried, the news cuts to the core of how she has been created by God. The sense of loss she feels is deep and profound. Her husband may experience some disappointment, but it is generally not the same kind of hurt that his wife is experiencing.

When I got the news that Mary Ann had miscarried, I was disappointed, but I was unprepared for how the news would affect Mary Ann. My initial reaction to her grief was to think to myself, *It's not that big a deal. We'll get pregnant again. She just needs to get over it.*

Wrong.

For a husband to love his wife incarnationally in a situation like this, he has to step into her world. He may not experience the same grief she experiences, but he can understand what it means to grieve. He must tenderly care for her in the midst of her sadness and not invalidate the depth of her emotions. Following the model of the Savior, he must become her sympathetic high priest (see Heb. 4:15) who knows her sorrow and helps her bear the burden.

Incarnational love means putting Romans 12:15 into practice: "Rejoice with those who rejoice, and weep with those who weep." We must be husbands who love and care for our wives even when we don't understand exactly what they're going through.

Sacrificial Love

There is a thin line that separates incarnational love from sacrificial love. In some ways, they are two sides of the same coin. Christ showed unconditional love by choosing us. He pledged His love for us in specific, covenantal terms. He demonstrated incarnational love by giving up the divine prerogative and coming into our world as a man. Ultimately, He showed that He was willing to give up more than the splendor of heaven; He showed His sacrificial love for us by willingly facing physical torture, shame and humiliation, and becoming the object of divine wrath as He gave up His life on the cross.

"God demonstrates His own love toward us," Paul writes, "in that while we were yet sinners, Christ died for us" (Rom. 5:8). For the deity to set aside some of His attributes and to dwell among us is an act of sacrifice. But for that same deity to willingly engineer the events of human history to allow Himself to be mocked, beaten, spat upon, stripped and nailed to a tree is the ultimate sacrifice. "Greater love has no one than this," Jesus says, "that one lay down his life for his friends" (John 15:13). In what is one of the most extraordinary statements in the Bible, Paul writes:

He made Him who knew no sin to be sin on our behalf, so that we might become the righteousness of God in Him (2 Cor. 5:21).

The death of Jesus on a cross outside Jerusalem almost 2,000 years ago is the defining event in human history. It is the supreme example of sacrificial love. In that light, it is almost startling for the apostle Paul to suggest that the kind of love a husband should express to his wife is the same kind of love Christ has for His Church. In fact, so we won't be confused, Paul completes his explanation by adding the phrase "and gave Himself up for her" (Eph. 5:25). As husbands, we have not begun to understand what it means to love our wives until we have experienced some kind of pain in the process.

We had been married five years when our marriage canoe traveled through some rough waters. The same week that I learned I had lost my job, we found out we were expecting our second child. After hunting for job options in the town where we were living, I ultimately decided my best option was to move our family to Phoenix. The house went on the market, and I headed to the desert to find a home for us in the Valley of the Sun. Along the way, I made some classic blunders:

- Mistake #1: Don't decide to buy a house your wife hasn't seen. I did. My priorities for what we needed weren't the same as my wife's priorities.
- Mistake #2: Don't leave your wife to pack and move all by herself in her fifth month of pregnancy. I did. The company was paying for the move, including packing the boxes. I figured there wasn't much work for her to do, so I stayed in Phoenix and waited for my wife and the moving van to arrive.
- Mistake #3: Don't underestimate the impact moving to a new city will have on a pregnant woman. Especially if she's moving a thousand miles away from her family and from the town where she grew up. Especially if she's moving to Phoenix in August.

Mary Ann arrived in Phoenix to find 110-degree heat, a house she hated and no one she knew. She became very depressed.

I would come home from work in the evenings to a silent wife and a three-year-old daughter. No dinner. Moving boxes throughout the house. "Let's go grocery shopping," I'd suggest in my cheeriest voice. We'd climb in the minivan and head to the store. "Let's get ice cream,"

I'd announce. Nothing seemed to break through the dark cloud that hovered around my wife's head. She even had no interest in watching the gymnastics competition in the Olympics that summer.

I had no idea what to do. I tried tackling projects I thought might help, like painting one of the rooms in the house. I pitched in by cooking, washing dishes, taking the family out to eat and doing whatever I could to help Mary Ann adjust to our new home.

After weeks of a lifeless, unresponsive reaction from my wife, I found myself walking through our backyard late one evening, crying out to God. "I don't know what to do," I told him. "I can't break through. I can't live like this. Help! This is no fun at all. I can see how people get to a point where they begin to think about divorce. I won't divorce her, but I don't know how long this can go on."

Why have you forsaken me? echoed through my mind as I realized where those words had come from. As He hung on His cross, pouring out His life to rescue His elect from an eternity in hell, Jesus cried out to God, saying, "'Eloi, Eloi, lama sabachthani?' which is translated, 'My God, My God, why have You forsaken Me?'" (Mark 15:34). Here I was, as a young husband, struggling at a difficult time in my marriage, wondering why I was suffering. In that moment, I realized my suffering, real as it was, did not compare with the suffering of Christ.

As I have shared this story at FamilyLife Marriage Conferences across the country, I've been approached by a number of couples who have had similar experiences. Some were still struggling with depression and difficult adjustments they were facing. "What did you do?" they asked. "How did you fix it?"

I wish I had an answer for them. Over time, our marriage made it to the other side of the rapids. God intervened and led us back into sunlight. Had the situation persisted, I would have sought counsel from our pastor. I would have turned to a doctor to see if there was any medical reason for Mary Ann's depression. I would have continued to cry out to God for wisdom and for direction.

Even in the midst of that difficult time, God was at work. He was using trials to build character in us (see Rom. 5:3-5; Jas. 1:2-4). I experienced His faithfulness in difficult times. I learned some lessons about moving, and I recommitted myself to loving my wife, even in the midst of personal pain. This was no time for me to focus on my needs or what I wanted from our relationship. My wife was struggling, and I needed to set aside any challenges I was facing in order to focus on helping her. It was time for sacrifice.

My lesson in sacrificial love is minor-league stuff. It pales in comparison to the kind of sacrificial love expressed by one of my heroes—a man I've never met but have admired from a distance. His name is Robertson McQuilkin.

McQuilkin had served for years as the president of Columbia Bible College and Seminary in Columbia, South Carolina, when his wife was diagnosed with Alzheimer's disease. He remembers the day he sat with her in the doctor's office, hoping and praying that a second opinion might turn up something different. His heart sank when the doctor asked his wife to name the four Gospels, and she looked pleadingly at him to help. McQuilkin remembers:

> I approached the college board of trustees with the need to begin the search for my successor. I told them that when the day came that Muriel needed me full-time, she would have me. I hoped that would not be necessary till I reached retirement, but at fifty-seven, it seemed unlikely I could hold on till sixty-five. . . .
>
> So began years of struggle with the question of what should be sacrificed: ministry or caring for Muriel. . . . When the time came, the decision was firm. It took no great calculation. It was a matter of integrity. Had I not promised, forty-two years before "in sickness and in health, till death do us part"?
>
> This was no grim duty to which I was stoically resigned, however. It was only fair. She had, after all, cared for me for almost four decades with marvelous devotion; now it was my turn. And such a partner she was! If I took care of her for forty years, I would never be out of her debt.[3]

McQuilkin's tender care for his wife is a reminder that it is often harder to live for your wife than it would be to die for her. It involves dying daily to your own desires and dreams. In the end, sacrificial love involves not only a willingness on the part of a husband to prefer his wife as more important than himself (see Phil. 2:3) but also a readiness to lay down everything he holds dear to care for her. It is a decision on the part of a husband that nothing will supersede his marriage covenant.

It's the kind of love that never gives up.

In Closing

Christ's love for His Church began in eternity past, before the foundation of the world, when He chose us as His adopted sons. He declared it for all time in a covenant. It was revealed in His incarnation, when He left the skybox of heaven for the bleachers of Earth to dwell among us. It reached its zenith in His willingness to suffer and die to redeem us.

A husband who would love his wife as Christ loved His Church will love her unconditionally, covenantally, incarnationally and sacrificially. In the process, he'll need to know the characteristics that will mark him as a great lover.

PointstoConsider

1. Read 1 John 3:16. What do you think it means "to lay down our lives for the brethren"? What do you think it means to lay down your life for your wife?
2. Read Ephesians 1:4-6. Why did Christ choose to adopt us as His sons? How would you compare this to the love you are to show for your wife?
3. What is significant about each type of unconditional love that a husband is to show his wife?

    • Covenantal love (see Gen. 15:8-21; Eccles. 5:4-5)
    • Incarnational love (see 1 John 4:9; Phil. 2:6-7)
    • Sacrificial love (see Rom. 5:8; John 15:13)

4. How can you display the following types of love in your marriage?

- Covenantal love
- Incarnational love
- Sacrificial love

CHAPTER 10

WHAT REAL LOVE LOOKS LIKE

If we attempted to construct a definition of love on the basis of popular song lyrics, we would not only wind up with terrible grammar but also with a very confused sense of what love is supposed to be. Most of us are shrewd enough to understand that the silly love songs we hear on the radio don't tell the whole story. Those romantic notions of what love is only tell a part of the story, if they tell any of the story at all.

We might come to that conclusion if we sat down to think long enough. But the constant bombardment of messages from popular culture continues to press relentlessly on our subconscious minds. It doesn't take long before we know intellectually that love is more than just warm feelings and attraction, but our operative definition of love has been reduced to little more than that.

It's no wonder, then, that a few years into a marriage a man might decide he doesn't "love" his wife anymore. He finds himself thinking, *You've lost that lovin' feeling, now it's gone, gone, gone, whoa-oh—oh.*

The ancient Greeks may have understood love better than we do. In their language, they used three different words to express different dimensions of love. The word *eros* described the passionate, physical and sexual expression of affection between two people. *Phileo* was the word they used to express companionship, friendship and the enjoyment felt when people were together with others whom shared common interests and values. *Agape* was their word for committed, self-sacrificing love that gives preference to others.

As you might expect, when Paul instructs a husband to love his wife as Christ loves the Church, he uses the last of those three Greek words. His command is not that we experience *eros*, although the Bible speaks clearly to that subject in other places. Likewise, he is not commanding us to be friends with each other, *phileo* love. The love a husband is commanded to have for his wife is an unselfish love that makes her needs more important than his own, which is *agape* love.

In our day, we need to stand against the cultural drumbeat that defines love in purely emotional or romantic terms. We need a renaissance of understanding what true love looks like. Thankfully, the Bible spells it out clearly for anyone who will listen. Husbands who want to love their wives as Christ loves His Church will be characterized by the kind of love Paul spells out in 1 Corinthians 13.

The Love Chapter

When I was in high school, everybody knew about 1 Corinthians 13. You could find the text of this chapter of the Bible printed on a poster and sold at a store that also sold posters of Jimi Hendrix and Led Zeppelin. You didn't have to be a Christian to know about the "love chapter." Everyone was into love.

What was promoted in the '60s as "free love" was neither free nor love. It was mostly self-indulgence. While it might have been hip to have a "love chapter" poster in your room, most people paid little attention to the call to self-sacrifice described in 1 Corinthians 13:

> Love is patient, love is kind and is not jealous; love does not brag and is not arrogant, does not act unbecomingly; it does not seek its own, is not provoked, does not take into account a wrong suffered, does not rejoice in unrighteousness, but rejoices with the truth; bears all things, believes all things, hopes all things, endures all things (vv. 4-7).

In one brief passage—fewer than 70 words—the apostle outlines 15 characteristics of love that stand in stark contrast to the kind of attitude most of his readers were expressing toward one another. There are seven positive statements about what love is and eight negative statements about what love is not.

Former Princeton theologian Charles Hodge offers this contrast. The characteristics of love Paul chose to highlight here, Hodge says, stand in opposition to the way in which the believers in Corinth were exhibiting their spiritual gifts:

> They were impatient, discontented, envious, inflated, selfish, indecorous, unmindful of the feelings or interests of others, suspicious, resentful, censorious.[1]

Paul's list here was not meant to be an exhaustive description of love; instead, it was offered in juxtaposition to what was being manifested in his day.

For us, the list provides husbands with a helpful tool for self-examination.

Love Is Patient and Kind

The story is told of a young Christian man, who asked an older believer to intercede for him. "Pray that I will grow in patience," the younger man asked earnestly. His friend suggested that they go to the Lord in prayer together, right then and there.

"Lord," the older man began, "I pray that you would bring trials and tribulation into Ben's life this very day. I pray he will experience trouble this morning and again this afternoon. I pray . . ."

The younger man interrupted his friend and said, "Wait, please! I wanted you to pray that I would grow in patience!"

The older man smiled, "That's what I was doing."

In the old days, we didn't dress up the word by calling it "patience." We called it what it really is. In older translations of this passage, you'll read, "love suffereth long" (*ASV*).

In Romans 5 and again in James 1, the Bible teaches that God brings trials in our life to help develop "endurance" or patience. Peter exhorted slaves to endure a harsh master with patience (see 1 Pet. 2:20). James told Christians who were being oppressed by the rich to bear up and to wait patiently for the coming of the Lord (see 5:7-8). He will judge our oppressor.

What happens to you when your wife inconveniences you? Do you become upset or angry when things don't turn out the way you expected they would? Are there habits she has that "get on your nerves"?

For example, do you struggle with patience when communicating with your wife? You ask about her day, and she tells you—in Technicolor, with footnotes! You even get some links to other sites in her brain along the way. And all the time, you're thinking, *Will you please land this plane! What's the point? What's the main idea?*

The root of impatience is usually selfishness. We're not getting what we want or what we think we deserve. We don't suffer long; rather, we think we've suffered long enough!

God's Word reminds us in the midst of our suffering that we haven't come close to enduring what He Himself has suffered. When He poured out His wrath on Sodom and Gomorrah, or when He destroyed the earth by flood, it wasn't because He lost His cool—it was His fair and righteous judgment on men for their unrepentant sin. What is remarkable is not that God chose to destroy the earth in the flood, but that He is so patient with all of us today.

When you think you've endured just about all you should have to endure, remember Jesus' example in 1 Peter 2:21-23:

For you have been called for this purpose, since Christ also suffered for you, leaving you an example for you to follow in His steps, who committed no sin, nor was any deceit found in His mouth; and while being reviled, He did not revile in return; while suffering, He uttered no threats, but kept entrusting Himself to Him who judges righteously.

"Patience," said Augustine, "is the companion of wisdom." An old, Dutch proverb acknowledges that the wise are not always patient, but that the patient are always wise: "A handful of patience is worth more than a bushel of brains."

A wise husband will show his love for his wife by patience.

Kindness is the flip side, which is active good will toward another person. In the book of Proverbs, kindness is often linked together with truth:

- Do not let kindness and truth leave you; bind them around your neck, write them on the tablet of your heart (3:3).
- Will they not go astray who devise evil? But kindness and truth will be to those who devise good (14:22).
- What is desirable in a man is his kindness, and it is better to be a poor man than a liar (19:22).
- She opens her mouth in wisdom, and the teaching of kindness is on her tongue (31:26).

Throughout the Psalms, the Bible talks about the "lovingkindness" of God. We are reminded that because of His mercy and lovingkindness, we have been redeemed. Again, we see kindness as actively doing something for our benefit.

Can you think of the last five things you've done for your wife that have been an expression of your kindness toward her? How have you affirmed her as your wife recently? How have you made her load lighter? Do you delight in doing acts of kindness toward her?

Do you respond with kindness even when she is impatient with you? In 1 Peter 3, you are instructed to live with your wife in an understanding manner, as fellow heirs of the grace of God; to be harmonious, sympathetic, brotherly, kindhearted, and humble, not returning evil for evil or insult for insult, but returning a blessing instead (see vv. 7-9). To love your wife well, you must be patient with her, and you must be kind.

Love Is Not Selfish

What the apostle Paul has already stated as a positive (love *is* patient and kind), he now restates as a negative (love *is not* arrogant, self-serving or jealous). Love is focused outward, away from us. So-called self-love is an oxymoron—it's really no love at all.

In our day, there's been a lot of talk about the need for people to have a healthy self-esteem and a positive self-image. Some have defended what amounts to little more than selfishness or self-absorption on the basis that the Bible teaches us that we must love ourselves. They point to Jesus' words in Matthew 22 and defend the idea of self-love:

> One of them, a lawyer, asked Him a question, testing Him, "Teacher, which is the great commandment in the Law?" And He said to him, "'You shall love the Lord your God with all your heart, and with all your soul, and with all your mind.' This is the great and foremost commandment. The second is like it, 'You shall love your neighbor as yourself'" (vv. 35-39).

"You see," they say, "the Bible teaches that if we are to love others, we must first love ourselves. Without a healthy self-esteem, we will never be able to love others the way we should."

Now, I believe we are to think rightly about ourselves. The Bible indeed teaches that we have been fearfully and wonderfully made. We are made in the very image of God. We have been created a little lower than the angels.

At the same time, the Bible teaches that we are all in Adam and have all been corrupted by the Fall. We are sinful, and the most obvious manifestation of our sinfulness is that we are selfish and self-absorbed. Knowing that we are made in the image of God and that we are the objects of His divine affection is not a cause for us to boast about our worth. It is instead another opportunity for us to marvel at the grace of our creator, who has chosen to love us in spite of our sin, not because of any intrinsic loveliness in our character or our nature.

Jesus was not commanding us to love ourselves, as some have suggested. He was calling us to love others in the same way that we already love ourselves. He was reminding us that our sin has caused us to be self-centered and self-focused. As a result of our sin, we now love ourselves. Jesus said the second greatest commandment is for us to love others with the same intensity.

A husband who loves his wife as Christ loved the Church will be selfless, not selfish. A selfish husband gets back from a weeklong business trip and insists on going to a sporting event with friends. He wants his wife to sit with him while he watches *SportsCenter*, but he refuses to sit still for one of her movies. He wants his wife to keep the kids quiet while he naps on Sunday, and he gets angry if the kids wake him up. It's all about him.

A selfless husband is always considering his wife's needs. He doesn't mind watching the kids while she enjoys an evening out with her friends. He even does the dishes after the kids are in bed. If he's in the mood for romance, he considers the kind of day she has had and does not insist that she be intimate with him. Rather than dwelling on his own needs, he considers her needs, too.

Selfless love, according to the Scriptures, is never envious or jealous. Here, of course, the Bible is warning us about the kind of destructive jealousy that wants control or ownership over another person. It's the kind of jealousy that has been called "the magnifier of trifles" and "the jaundice of the soul." "Wrath is fierce and anger is a flood, but who can stand before jealousy?" asks Proverbs 27:4.

We've all heard the stories of the jealous husband. Fueled by his own insecurities and emotional scars, he becomes enraged over any innocent action by his wife that he perceives as a threat. His jealousy will lead him to become emotionally and perhaps even physically abusive. One husband I know described his own struggle with jealousy:

If my wife was going to the store, I had to know exactly what she needed to buy. I calculated how long it should take her to go and come back. I grilled her about anyone she had seen while she was there. If it took her five minutes longer than I thought it should, I would become enraged.

That's not love. That is sinful, selfish insecurity being expressed in hostility against another person.

God is a jealous God. His perfect jealousy is motivated by His love for us and by His desire that we love Him more than anyone or anything else. Yet He does not need our love. He is jealous for our benefit, not for His own. As husbands, we ought to be jealous to protect our covenant relationship with our wives. But as soon as that healthy, protective care for our relationship is infected by our own selfishness, it can turn from godly jealousy to a dangerous, sinful brew.

Another of the selfish characteristics that is antithetical to real love is arrogance and boasting. Once again, fueled by insecurity, a man will seek to exalt himself in the eyes of others. He will not only feel superior to others, he will look for opportunities to express his superiority. Rather than following the example of Christ, who showed His love for us when He humbled Himself, the arrogant man will show his contempt for others by thinking more highly of himself and his abilities than he ought.

An arrogant husband will have no regard for his wife's wisdom, her gifts, her skills or her value. He will not seek her input. He will claim his right to "lead" the relationship. If things go wrong, he will often find a reason to blame his mate for the failure. He "stirs up strife," according to Proverbs 28:25. "The fear of the LORD is to hate evil; pride and arrogance and the evil way and the perverted mouth, I hate" (Prov. 8:13).

The opposite of arrogance is humility. The humble husband will recognize and quickly acknowledge the help he receives from his wife. Recently, I spoke with the wife of a noted Christian leader. In almost 40 years of ministry, this man has toured the world, speaking out for Christ. He has written best-selling books. The day we spoke, he had arrived home from a week of traveling and asked his wife what she thought about his taking off on another unplanned trip the following day.

Many wives would become bitter if their husbands kept that kind of schedule. I asked this man's wife how she handled his activity and his travel. "I know I'm his top priority," she said confidently. "Every day, he affirms me, he brags on me and he lets me know he loves me. When I know that he cares about me more than anyone or anything else, it's a lot easier to cheer him on when he leaves on another trip."

An arrogant husband does whatever he wants to do. A humble husband lets his wife know that she is his top priority. She has seen him put his schedule on hold to care for her when she really needs him. He puts her first.

The Bible also describes a loving person as one who does not act unbecomingly. This is about more than just good manners. A man who is characterized by love is not rude or inconsiderate of those around him. He is gracious and seeks to make others feel comfortable.

In almost two decades of marriage, there have been a number of times when I have found myself on the way home with my wife in a very quiet car after an evening with friends. "Is something wrong?" I have innocently asked, only to have my wife point back to something I said or did earlier in the evening and say, "You embarrassed me."

Usually, at that moment, I'll think to myself, *She's being too sensitive*. I'll excuse my actions by saying, "I didn't mean to," as if my lack of malicious intent should excuse the crime.

In those instances, I have typically been guilty of acting in an unbecoming way. Even if I think my behavior was not particularly offensive, the fact that I acted without thinking about how my behavior might make my wife feel is enough to qualify my actions as inconsiderate.

A few years ago, our church was considering a certain young man as a possible youth pastor. One Sunday evening, he and his wife shared their testimony of faith in Christ with our congregation, and we were invited to ask questions. Never shy, I raised my hand and asked, "Tell us about the first time you kissed your wife."

If I had taken a few extra minutes to think, I might have realized that the question was not appropriate in that setting. It may have been a fair question for the members of the search committee to ask in private, but it was out of line for me in the middle of the Sunday evening service!

My "unbecoming" question embarrassed my wife—and rightly so. A loving husband will not only be gracious and considerate when his wife is with him, but he also will want his behavior to be exemplary at all times. Unbecoming actions can be an embarrassment to his mate, even if she is not present at the time. Such inconsiderate behavior is out of sync with the biblical idea of what love is.

Paul sums up the idea that love is not jealous, boastful, arrogant or inconsiderate by saying, "It does not seek its own" (1 Cor. 13:5). At the root of all sin is our preoccupation with self. Bible commentator R. C. H. Lenski has said, "Cure selfishness and you have just replanted the Garden of Eden."[2]

I don't remember where I saw it first, but I came across a list with a curious title. It was labeled, "How to Make Yourself Perfectly Miserable," and it offered the following suggestions:

1. Think about yourself.
2. Talk about yourself.
3. Use the personal pronoun "I" as often as possible in your conversation.
4. Mirror yourself continually in the opinion of others.
5. Listen greedily to what people say about you.
6. Insist on consideration and respect.
7. Demand agreement with your own views on everything.
8. Sulk if people are not grateful to you for favors shown them.
9. Never forget a service you may have rendered.
10. Expect to be appreciated.
11. Be suspicious.
12. Be sensitive to slights.
13. Be jealous and envious.
14. Never forget a criticism.
15. Trust nobody but yourself.

As a husband reads back over that list, he must ask himself if any of those characteristics might hit a little close to home. They mark the antithesis of the humble Christ, and as such, they stand in contrast to the character of a man who loves his wife as Christ loves His Church.

Love Is Not Easily Offended

I remember my mother describing people she knew as "thin-skinned." It was not a compliment. These people wounded easily, bruised easily and bled easily. You had to walk softly around them, especially if they were in one of their moods. You never knew what would provoke their anger, tears or silence.

A loving husband will need to acquire an extra layer of calluses on his skin. If he is to love his wife as Christ loved the Church, then according to the Scriptures, he must not be easily provoked.

To understand what this means, think of the kind of dog you'd like to own, especially if you have young children. If your dog growls, snaps and nips at you anytime he is startled, he's probably not a candidate for pooch-of-the-year at your house. You want the kind of dog that can withstand the tail pulling of a spiteful child without bearing so much as a fang. You want a calm, gentle dog who is at ease in the midst of confusion.

In the same way, a loving husband is not to be easily stirred to anger. That doesn't mean a husband will never be angry. Jesus got angry when he saw His Father's house turned into a supermarket. He grabbed a stick and drove men out of the Temple. He was righteously indignant (see Matt. 21:12-16).

This same man, just a few days later, was to be falsely accused of blasphemy, and then beaten, mocked, spat upon, stripped naked and nailed to a cross. In the face of that kind of ridicule and abuse, He did not respond in anger. He responded with silence, uttering no threats, and entrusting Himself to Him who judges rightly (see 1 Pet. 2:23).

The reason Christ displayed godly anger in one instance and godly forbearance in the other was, at least in part, the object of the ridicule. In the first instance, the worship of God was being mocked by men who had turned it into a way to make money. However, when He faced His own scourging, Jesus knew His silent suffering would ultimately bring glory to God. His anger at the Temple had nothing to do with personal inconveniences or offenses, but was only stirred when He saw God being mocked.

Paul makes this contrast clear when he describes love as being not easily provoked and then quickly adds that it does not rejoice in unrighteousness. Paul acknowledges that there is an appropriate expression of anger that is stirred when you see someone else suffering unjustly or when God's reputation is impugned. "In your anger," the apostle says, "do not sin." (Eph. 4:26, *NIV*). In other words, if your anger is stirred by the unrighteousness of men, and if God's reputation is being dragged through the mud and you get angry about it, don't let your anger cause us to sin. As for you, when people try to provoke you to anger, shake it off.

In marriage, there will be times when your mate provokes, annoys, angers, frustrates, perturbs—you get the idea. In some cases, it will be unintentional. In other cases, your wife may be expressing legitimate frustration or anger about things you've done or left undone. There will be times when conflict arises. The godly husband, according to the Scriptures, will not be easily provoked.

He will also not be a husband who documents and catalogs every time his wife wrongs him. Love, according to the Scriptures, does not take into account a wrong suffered. Here, Paul uses a bookkeeping term to indicate that love does not keep a ledger of offenses.

In Matthew 18, where Peter asks Jesus if he ought to forgive his brother as many as seven times for an offense, he uses a number that, in the Jewish mind, signified completion. God created the world in seven days. Joshua marched around Jericho seven times. Peter is, in essence, asking, "Do I forgive him completely?"

Jesus' response is classic. His "seventy times seven" formula is Jesus' way of saying, "If you're keeping count, you're not forgiving! Forgive your brother until you've lost count of the number of times you've done it."

We should keep no record of wrongs. We must give up what we falsely think is our right to punish the other person for the way they have offended us. As someone has said When we bury the hatchet, we've got to make sure we don't leave the handle sticking out of the ground so we can grab it again the next time we need it!

Ruth Bell Graham has said that a successful marriage is the union of two forgivers. She's right. A loving husband will be quick to forgive and move on.

Love Bears, Believes, Hopes and Endures

Paul concludes his description of the characteristics of love with a summary statement:

> Love "bears all things, believes all things, hopes all things, endures all things" (1 Cor. 13:7).

A husband who wants to love his wife well must learn what it means to bear, believe, hope and endure.

Some may think the Scriptures contradict themselves here. On one hand, we are told to bear all things; in another place, Paul chastises the Corinthians for a lack of discernment. "For you tolerate it if anyone," he says, "enslaves you, anyone devours you, anyone takes advantage of you, anyone exalts himself, anyone hits you in the face" (2 Cor. 11:20). Paul is not praising them here for their patience; instead, he is suggesting that their actions are foolish.

Again, when Paul teaches us to "believe all things," one has to remember his stinging rebuke of false teachers. He certainly did not want the Galatians to believe the false gospel being propagated by the Judaizers:

> But even if we, or an angel from heaven, should preach to you a gospel contrary to what we have preached to you, he is to be accursed! As we have said before, so I say again now, if any man is preaching to you a gospel contrary to what you received, he is to be accursed! (Gal. 1:8-9).

He has just stated that love rejoices in the truth. When he instructs us to believe all things, he would not want us to be led into error.

In the same way, his charge to hope all things and endure all things must be understood in context. This is another scriptural example where "all" doesn't mean "every single thing." God wants us to be characterized by these qualities but not to apply them universally in every situation.

What does it mean to "bear all things"? The Word itself has two connotations in the text. First, it can mean to assume the weight of something. This is the meaning Paul has in mind when he says, "Now we who are strong ought to bear the weaknesses of those without strength and not just please ourselves" (Rom. 15:1).

The word "bear" can also mean "to cover." Peter explains it this way: "Above all, keep fervent in your love for one another, because love covers a multitude of sins" (1 Pet. 4:8). "Cover" here does not mean "cover up," but "cover over." Jews would have understood this easily, knowing that the blood of the atonement that was sprinkled on the mercy seat was meant as a covering for the sins of the people (see Lev. 16:14). In the same way, the Messiah, according to Isaiah's prophecy, would be the One who bears our griefs and carries our sorrows (see Isa. 53:4).

Therefore, a husband will love his wife by first bearing the weight of the responsibility for his marriage and his family. He will be the one who bears the weight of their financial needs. He will bear the weight of her emotional needs. He will bear the weight in those times when someone must apply godly wisdom in decision-making. As much as possible, he will remove the burdens of life from his wife's shoulders, leading her to the feet of the Savior, where together they may cast their burdens on Him.

Additionally, a husband will show his love for his wife by covering over her sins and her faults. In the same way that two of Noah's sons covered the shame of their father's nakedness after he had become drunk (see Gen. 9:23), a husband will be gracious in covering "a multitude of sins." This is what it means to "bear all things."

Next, Paul says we are to "believe all things." Rather than suggesting that we be gullible, Paul means that we are to be trusting and not suspicious by nature. In marriage, the basis for our trust is our covenant relationship with each other. We can trust one another in the day-to-day activities of life because our relationship is founded on a pledge we have made to each other, which we have never threatened to violate or dissolve.

Here is the place where we ought to apply what theologian R. C. Sproul has called "the judgment of charity." In every situation, Sproul says, we as believers are to assign the highest and best possible motives to the actions of another person, until the evidence indicates otherwise. Bible teacher Henry Ironside says it this way:

Love may see something upon which a very bad construction may be put, but it waits a moment and says, "could I put a better construction upon that?" I will not put the wrong one if I can possibly find a good one.[3]

John MacArthur adds:

If there is doubt about a person's guilt or motivation, love will always opt for the most favorable possibility. If a loved one is accused of something wrong, love will consider him innocent until proven guilty. If he turns out to be guilty, love will give credit for the best motive.[4]

I saw this principle illustrated in high school in a way I have never forgotten. I was standing by my locker on the second floor, right outside Mr. Richard's room, talking to Marcy, when a group of girls passed by. They were talking loudly and making a commotion. When one of them saw Marcy, she made some tacky remark about her to her friends, in a voice that was loud enough for everyone in the hall to hear it, including Marcy.

I don't remember what she said, but I've never forgotten Marcy's response. After spinning around to see who had made the remark, I turned to look at Marcy to see what she would do. Would she start crying? Would she shout something back? I half expected a Roller Derby-styled hallway fight might break out between two high school girls.

None of that happened. Instead, Marcy registered a stunned look for a minute. Then she blinked, looked at me, smiled and said, "She must be having a really bad day."

A bad day? I thought to myself, *Give me a break!* This girl has watched *Pollyanna* one too many times! But that scene has been etched in my mind ever since that day as a reminder of how to apply the judgment of charity.

For us as husband, the command to believe all things means to be building, establishing and pursuing a relationship founded in trust. It means we must first be trustworthy men. We must not be characterized by suspicion. And when our trust is violated, we must design a way to restore it.

We are also to be hopeful men. Not only do we believe the best about another person, but we also hope for the best as well. It is a biblical call to be prayerfully optimistic.

Most of the time when the Bible speaks about hope, it points us to our ultimate hope—that Christ will return and that His Bride will live with Him in heaven forever. But when we rightly understand the sovereignty of God in all situations, we have great hope. Not only do we have hope for the future, but we also have confidence that even in the midst of present difficulty and adversity, God knows what He's doing, and His plan will not be thwarted.

I am by nature an optimist. Mary Ann has to remind me on occasion that my optimism needs to be balanced by her "realism." (She insists she is not a pessimist but a realist!) Being hopeful does not mean believing that Jesus was just kidding when he said, "In the world you have tribulation" (John 16:33). Having hope means that we finish that verse: "Take courage; I have overcome the world."

I have often wondered how men without hope ultimately survive in a fallen world. What keeps them going in the midst of difficult circumstances? Without a quiet confidence that God is in control of His universe, what keeps them from despair? A man who is hopeful expresses his love for his wife by continuing to remind her of the sovereignty of God in the face of adversity.

One night, years ago, I sat with two friends who were ready to end their marriage. For some time, Jeff had been suffering the effects of chronic fatigue syndrome. As his condition got worse, he grew more concerned about his ability to keep his job and to provide for his family. The stress on their marriage grew, and neither one knew how to cope with it.

Jeff and Robin were angry at each other. Jeff wanted control. Money became a huge issue. Jeff pinched pennies, fearing he might lose his job at any time. He expected Robin to manage the household on an extremely tight budget. He felt overwhelmed by the responsibilities of being a husband and a father.

Robin wanted freedom. She was tired of taking the kids out for dinner and a movie, only to face Jeff's anger for having squandered his hard-earned money. She didn't understand the increased pressure her husband was feeling. She wanted the pain and the loneliness to end. She was looking for some way, any way, to escape. The absence of real marital intimacy left her empty. She attempted to fill the emotional void with food and consequently put on weight. Ultimately, she found solace in alcohol.

As I sat with this couple at church on a Wednesday night while their three girls were at Awana, I saw very little hope left for this marriage. Both were too exhausted or too ill equipped to try anymore. Neither one cared about the other's feelings. Their plan was to separate, even though they knew that most separations end in divorce.

As we talked about their marriage that night, I looked at both of them and said, "Do you know what I'm hoping for? I'm hoping that five years from tonight, you might be able to stand in front of a group of people, telling them your story. I'm hoping that you'll be able to look back on this night and say, 'God resurrected our marriage. We want to testify to his goodness.' I believe that's what God wants, and that's what I'm hoping will happen."

A year later, Jeff and Robin's marriage did end. She had the freedom she wanted, and he had control over his life. He traveled, saw friends, stayed with relatives and indulged his passion—watching trains. Robin began her new life as a single mom with three girls. She sold the house, moved to a new town and kept her drinking problem hidden from everyone.

Over the next several months, however, God began to work in Jeff's heart and in Robin's heart. The end of the marriage had not provided them with a quick fix for their problems. They knew they had violated their covenant by getting a divorce. Jeff was beginning to see his own selfishness and need for control. Robin's drinking was beginning to scare her. God was at work in their lives, unearthing and revealing sin, bringing both of them to a place of brokenness and repentance.

When Robin called and asked Jeff about exploring the option of reconciliation, he was open but skeptical. The divorce had not brought either of them what they really wanted. Jeff knew the odds were against them. He also knew that divorce was not God's will for them. Cautiously, the couple began to explore the options for putting their marriage back together.

God blessed their obedience. Over the next year, the Holy Spirit brought them face-to-face with their selfishness and their sin. They saw clearly how they had failed one another. Instead of concentrating on each other's faults, Jeff and Robin began to focus on the part they had individually played in the disintegration of their marriage.

Today, almost five years later, Jeff and Robin are husband and wife again. They continue to wrestle with patterns from the past, but there is a new willingness to listen and understand each other. Jeff has surrendered his need for control and learned to trust in God's sovereignty. Robin is sober. She has learned to embrace her emotions, as scary as they may be, instead of trying to kill them with alcohol or binge eating. They have a ministry to couples in their church who are facing challenges in their marriage. Jeff told me recently, "Any problem these couples are facing, we've been through! We provide them with a living illustration that no matter how bad your marriage is, it can survive and even thrive if your faith is in Christ."

I asked Jeff during that conversation if he remembered what I had told him the first time we met about God using their broken marriage to bring glory to Himself. He remembered. That vision—that hope—had helped bring a dead marriage back to life.

Are you a hopeful husband? Is your first impulse in the ebb and flow of daily living to be positive and optimistic? Would your wife characterize you as a hopeful person? If not, ask yourself these questions:

1. What is it about God's plan for me and my family that I don't like or don't trust?
2. Can I see the hand of God at work in the middle of my circumstances?
3. Do I believe He is working everything for my good, as He has promised to do (see Rom. 8:28)?

When the answer to those questions is "yes," there is great reason for hope.

Finally, Paul says, love "endures all things." Like soldiers holding a strategic post in the midst of battle, love will stand firm no matter who attacks. The word used by Paul here is a military term that means "to sustain the attack of an enemy." When circumstances are unbearable, love won't quit. When it's hard to believe in anything anymore, love hangs tough. When things are hopeless, love doesn't give up. Love endures.

In fact, this is the quality of love that proves all the others Paul has talked about. Roy Laurin asks:

> What good is patience, kindness, generosity, humility, courtesy, unselfishness, good nature, charitableness, sincerity, goodness, graciousness, confidence and assurance unless they continue? Most of us can be kind for a day, but love is kindness that endures. Most of us can be patient for a while, but love is patience that endures.[5]

The foundation of a marriage relationship is a vow made by a husband and a wife to each other. In that vow, both promise before God to endure. "What about in sickness?" the preacher asks. "What about in poverty? What about when things take a turn for the worse? What then?" At that moment, before God and man, a husband looks deeply into the eyes of the woman about to become his wife and says, "Only one thing will ever separate me from you, and that's death. Until then, I promise I will love, honor and cherish you. I promise I will endure."

Sadly, too many of those same husbands renege on that promise. They swore they would forsake all others, but someone comes along and they forget their vow. Or they get tired of the responsibilities of being a husband, and they abandon their promise. When the enemy presses in, they leave their post.

That man is a fraud. He has taken lightly the vow he made before God. It is right for us to ask why we ought to trust anything else he might promise to say or do. He may have faithfully fulfilled his assignment to love at every point, but if he fails here, all of his previous successes count for nothing. A man may lose patience and recover. He may speak unkindly and be forgiven. He may take his hand off the wheel and find his way back on the road. But a man who fails to endure has failed to love.

In Closing

Love is hard work. It demands that a husband be patient and kind. He is not selfish or arrogant. He always takes into consideration how his actions will reflect on his mate. He keeps his anger under control and is quick to forgive. He is committed to godliness and truth. He carries the weight. He trusts his wife. He is hopeful and optimistic. And he keeps on loving, no matter what. Are you man enough to be a loving husband? You are if you're God's man.

PointstoConsider

1. The Greeks used three different words to express different dimensions of love. What do each of these three words mean?

   - *Eros*
   - *Phileo*
   - *Agape*

2. First Corinthians 13 is called "The Love Chapter." In this chapter, Paul presents a call to *agape* love, a love of self-sacrifice. For each of the following phrases from 1 Corinthians 13, look up the corresponding Scripture and then write down some ways you can practically apply this truth in your marriage.

   Love:

   - Is patient (see 1 Pet. 2:21-23)
   - Is kind (see Prov. 3:3)

- Does not brag and is not arrogant (see Matt. 22:35-39)
- Is not provoked, does not take into account a wrong suffered (see 1 Pet. 2:23)
- Bears all things, believes all things, hopes all things, endures all things (see 1 Pet. 4:8; Rom. 8:28)

CHAPTER 11

THE GOAL OF LOVE

Your mission, Jim, should you decide to accept it . . .

One of the pop-culture clichés of my generation came from the opening of the *Mission: Impossible* television series that aired from 1966-1972. Each week, agent Jim Phelps would switch on his ultramodern, state-of-the-art mini reel-to-reel tape recorder to hear his new assignment. He and his team of covert operatives were asked each week to do the impossible and to save the world from doom. The tape ended with the ominous warning that if any agents were caught, the government would disavow any knowledge of their mission. Five seconds later, the tape was a puff of smoke.

Jim and his team were highly qualified and specially trained to do their jobs. But it was their goal that kept them willing to face danger and death each week. While all of us were sleeping soundly in our beds, the

IMF team kept the world safe for us, thwarting the hostile and insidious plans of enemies and terrorists around the globe.

As we've already seen, a husband must also be both qualified and trained for his assignment. He must understand and embrace the unique way God has created him as a man. He must discipline himself for the purpose of godliness. He must assume his role by being a sympathetic priest, a courageous prophet and a king whose reign is characterized by self-sacrifice and responsibility. His mission, as outlined in Scripture, is to love his wife. If he'd had a mini reel-to-reel tape recorder of his own, the apostle Paul would have described a husband's assignment with these familiar words from the New Testament:

> Husbands, love your wives, just as Christ also loved the church and gave Himself up for her, so that He might sanctify her, having cleansed her by the washing of water with the word, that He might present to Himself the church in all her glory, having no spot or wrinkle or any such thing; but that she would be holy and blameless. So husbands ought also to love their own wives as their own bodies. He who loves his own wife loves himself; for no one ever hated his own flesh, but nourishes and cherishes it, just as Christ also does the church, because we are members of His body (Eph. 5:25-30).

We've already seen what it means to love our wives. What many of us have never stopped to consider, though, is the *goal* of our love. Why did God command it? If our assignment is to love our wives, what is that love supposed to accomplish?

In our day, a growing number of Christian men could clearly state that they are responsible before God to love their wives as Christ also loved the Church. They could even go the next step and explain that Christ demonstrated His love for the Church, according to Ephesians 5, by giving Himself up for her.

But ask those same men *why* they are to love their wives and, for the most part, you'll get a blank stare. Ask them about their responsibility to be used by God as agents of sanctification for their wives, and they won't have a clue what you're talking about. Ask them what it means to nourish and cherish their wives according to the mandate of Scripture, and most men will be speechless.

Agents of Sanctification

If I understand what Paul is teaching in the passage above, a part of my assignment, as a husband, is to be a sanctifying influence on my wife. The model for how I am to do this is Christ. He demonstrated His love for us by His willingness to suffer and die for us (see Rom. 5:8). By His death, He has redeemed us from the curse of the law (see Gal. 3:13). But He didn't stop there. He gave Himself for us that He might sanctify us (see Eph. 5:26), and so that we might be conformed to the image of Christ (see Rom. 8:29). In other words, Jesus loved us and died for us so that He could begin His work in us, making us into the kind of godly and holy men and women He wants us to be.

In the same way, I believe God is challenging us as husbands to be agents of sanctification—to assist Him in the sanctifying work He is doing in our wives' lives. My sacrificial love for my wife is to have a purpose. It's not her happiness but her holiness that should direct how I am to love and lead her. I should be committed to God's purpose in her life, even if I have to lay down my own life in the process.

I wish I could say that over the last 20 years I have understood and applied what the Scriptures seem to teach here. The truth is, I've been caught in the same cultural undertow that most other husbands have experienced. I have known and embraced my responsibility as a husband to love my wife. Too often, though, I've confused pleasing my wife with loving her. Instead of loving her by pressing her toward God's plan for her life, I've too often assumed that loving her meant sacrificing what I want and letting her have her way.

All of us who are a part of the Body of Christ are charged with the responsibility to "stimulate one another to love and good deeds" (Heb. 10:24). And all of us are responsible as individuals to respond to the sanctifying work of the Holy Spirit in our lives. It is God the Holy Spirit who is at work in us, making us more like Christ. He is the ultimate agent of sanctification.

Still, God has invited us as husbands to join Him in the work of sanctification by loving our wives in a way that will draw them closer to Him. The Holy Spirit is in charge of the mission, but we're on the team. When we said, "I do," this is a part of what we agreed to.

Exemplary Behavior

How do we carry out our assignment? How can we as husbands be a sanctifying influence on our wives? In a broad sense, our character, our behavior and our choices will have a subtle impact on our wives. As we live a godly life and make godly choices, we will be influencing them by the example we set.

Loving our wives in this way, then, will mean that we are both *models* and *promoters* of truth and righteousness. As men, we should not be leading our wives into sin—we should be taking their hands and leading them in the opposite direction.

Imagine your wife on a game show patterned after *The Newlywed Game*, called *What Would Your Husband Do?* The host asks questions of the wives, presenting them with moral dilemmas, which always lead up to the question: "In that situation, what would your husband do?" A wife ought to be able to win that game show every time, stating with confidence that in any situation her husband would do whatever is true, righteous and godly. As an act of love for her, your actions ought to be exemplary and above reproach. This provides her with a great sense of trust and security.

Shortly after Mary Ann and I started dating, we were sitting together at a Bible study. The study leader was teaching on assurance of our salvation, and he made a passing reference to our being "sealed by the spirit of promise." He didn't cite the verse to which he was referring (it's found in Ephesians 1:13), but I watched out of the corner of my eye as my companion turned right to the verse!

I was stunned! How did she know where that verse was found? Like most people, I knew John 3:16 and maybe a handful of other verses. But this young lady had turned right to some obscure reference in Ephesians, of all places.

I later learned that Mary Ann had been urged to memorize dozens of Bible verses during her first two years as a Christian. She had purposefully set about the task of memorizing a number of passages that reinforced basic truths about the Christian life. Not only had I never heard of such a thing (no one memorized Bible verses in the church I went to when I was growing up), but I also found myself a little intimidated by this young lady who knew more about the Bible than I did.

Mary Ann wasn't showing off. And she wasn't trying to make a point with me. She was simply living out her Christianity in front of me. Without even realizing it, she was having a sanctifying influence on me. I was challenged by her discipline and devotion to God and to the study of His Word. Here I was, supposed to be leading our relationship spiritually, and the woman I was supposed to be leading was miles ahead of me!

The Bible encourages wives to have this kind of sanctifying influence on their husbands, particularly if their husband has not been converted to Christ. "Wives," Peter says, "be submissive to your own husbands so that even if any of them are disobedient to the word, they may be won without a word by the behavior of their wives, as they observe your chaste and respectful behavior" (1 Pet. 3:1-2). In other words, Peter says, by living a godly life in front of her husband, a wife can be an agent of sanctification in his life.

In the same way, a husband's behavior ought to be exemplary. His wife ought to be challenged in her own spiritual life by the model and example of her husband. His high moral standards, courage and character should stimulate her to live the same kind of life before God.

But the assignment is different for men. God may use a wife's quiet and submissive spirit in her husband's life, but her core role as a wife does not involve spiritual leadership. She *may* influence him by her behavior, but he must assume the responsibility to nurture and disciple her. It's at the core of what it means to be a husband. While wives are called to let their example be a passive influence on their husbands, God calls a man to an active role. He must begin by setting a godly example, but he is not to stop there. Following the example of Christ, a husband ought to sanctify his wife by cleansing her (see Eph. 5:26), by nourishing her and by cherishing her (see v. 29).

Cleansing Agent

It was a custom in ancient times for a bride to be bathed before her wedding. The custom was not simply carried out for aesthetic purposes. That bath had the same symbolic idea as a white wedding gown. The freshly bathed bride would arrive at the altar pure and clean. She would be, in the language of Ephesians 5, "having no spot or wrinkle or any such thing" (v. 27). Any impurity or defilement that might have existed was figuratively washed away in that prenuptial bath.

In the same way, when a man confesses his sins and comes to Christ, he is cleansed from all unrighteousness. Old things are passed away, and all things are made new (see 2 Cor. 5:17). Our Bridegroom washes us with His blood, and we publicly declare that we are His in a covenant cleansing ceremony of our own—baptism.

There is a significant difference between the ancient custom of a wedding day bath and the cleansing of the Bride spoken of in Ephesians 5. In the first case, the bride makes herself ready for her husband. But in the Scriptures, the Bride of Christ is incapable of cleansing herself. It is her Beloved who cleanses her, with His own blood, and who washes her in water with the Word.

Now, in a very real sense, God the Holy Spirit is the agent of sanctification in the life of every believer. He is the One who is charged with the responsibility of conforming us to the image of Christ. Although His ministry to us is sometimes direct and personal, He often chooses to work through the lives of other believers to press us toward holiness.

According to this passage, then, God wants a husband to follow the example of Christ and to take responsibility for his wife's spiritual growth. John MacArthur says:

> [Just as] saving grace makes believers holy through the cleansing agency of the Word of God . . . it is with that same purpose and in that same love that husbands are to cultivate the purity, righteousness, and sanctity of their wives.[1]

Or, as James Boice says, "God holds husbands responsible for the spiritual growth and maturing of their wives."[2]

This responsibility for my wife's spiritual growth involves two primary assignments: I am not to lead her into sin, and I am to lead her into righteousness.

A few years back, I was a guest on a radio talk show, fielding calls from listeners about marriage. A young woman who called in that day said that she and her husband were having marital problems. As she explained it to me, there were sexual practices he wanted her to engage in which are clearly forbidden in Scripture, including the two of them viewing pornography together. He was angry with her because of her refusal, and she called me, wondering if she should submit to him in these practices. She told me that her husband claimed to be a follower of Christ.

The only way a husband can lead his wife into sin is if he is going there himself. I believe there are many husbands today who attempt to justify their own sinful behavior by trying to get their wives to join them in it. I told this caller that a wife is never to obey her husband if he asks her to violate the commands of God. In this case, I suggested that she seek counsel from her pastor, asking him if he thought she ought to participate in these activities. My hope was not only to direct her to ongoing godly counsel, but also to expose her husband's sin in hopes that the Church would confront him and hold him accountable.

In Genesis 12, we read about a husband who led his wife into sin. The father of the nation of Israel, Abraham, began his patriarchal career by asking his wife to tell a little white lie.

Abram and his wife Sarai had gone to Egypt to find food, for there was a famine in the land where God had brought them. Abram was afraid that some Egyptian man would find Sarai attractive and would kill him so that he might have her for his wife, so Abram instructed Sarai to lie and to say she was his sister.

Now, whom was Abram worried about? Not Sarai. He wanted to protect his own skin. Since everyone thought Sarai was Abram's sister, all the Egyptian men figured she was fair game. She was taken to Pharaoh's house and was about to become a part of the harem when God stepped in. He sent a plague on the house of Pharaoh and made it known to Pharaoh that Sarai was a married woman.

Pharaoh was not happy with Abram for perpetrating this hoax. In the providence of God, Abram and Sarai were able to get out of Egypt alive.

Whether it involves viewing pornography or telling a lie, like asking your wife to sign a dishonest income tax return, a husband who encourages his wife to sin is falling short of the example of Christ. We are called to live holy and blameless lives, and to invite our wives to follow us as we follow Christ.

As we turn away from sin, we are also to lead our wives in the paths of righteousness for His name's sake. This involves active encouragement and discipleship as we seek to see our wives grow in their walk with the Lord.

There are three primary ways in which we can encourage our wives to grow. The first is to do all we can to help them grow in their personal walk with Christ. We should help provide time for our wives to be in prayer and in their study of God's Word. We can point them to resources for this and can suggest other books to read or audiocassettes to listen to. We can also make it possible for them to have extended times away for personal retreat and solitude.

Second, we ought to take the initiative and encourage them to grow with us. We should set aside time to read with them, and to pray and study together. Some husbands I know make it a practice to read a book together at night, before bed, taking turns reading the chapters out loud. Another friend sets aside a three-hour chunk of time each week for reading and studying together with his wife. Even a one-page devotional each day will give you an opportunity to grow together.

Finally, we can lead our wives to corporate worship. We should be the ones leading them to participate in Sunday worship, as well as Bible studies and fellowship with other believers. We should make possible the opportunity for them to be a part of women's Bible study groups. It is our responsibility to make sure our wives and we have plenty of opportunity to grow in our relationship with Christ. And if our wives have a question about the Scriptures, we need to stand ready to help them find the answer (see 1 Cor. 14:35).

Christ has cleansed us, the Bible teaches, "by the washing of water with the word" (Eph. 5:26). Most Bible scholars believe that verse is a reference to our baptism and to our profession of faith. The writer of Hebrews, however, has a different kind of cleansing in mind when he talks about how drawing near to Christ leads to our sanctification:

> "Since we have a great priest over the house of God," he says, "let us draw near with a sincere heart in full assurance of faith, having our hearts sprinkled clean from an evil conscience and our bodies washed with pure water" (10:21-22).

In John 17, Jesus prays for His followers that God will "sanctify them in the truth" (v. 17). God uses His truth—His Word—as His means of grace to make us more like Himself. In that way, God's Word is like water: the more we're immersed in it, the more it does its work of cleansing us and making us more like Christ. As we read, study, meditate and memorize on God's Word, He will use His Word to change us. That's why Paul exhorts us to "let the word of Christ richly dwell within you, with all wisdom teaching and admonishing one another" (Col. 3:16), and why David reminds us, "Your word I have treasured in my heart, that I may not sin against You" (Ps. 119:11).

John MacArthur puts it this way:

> Men, if you love a woman, you will do everything in your power to maintain her holiness, her virtue, her righteousness, and her purity . . . every day you live. You'll never put her in a compromising situation where she would become angered, because that's a sin. You would never induce an argument out of her, because that's a sin. You would do nothing to defile her. You would never let her see anything or expose her to anything, or let her indulge in anything that would in any way bring impurity into her life. Love always seeks to purify.[3]

A husband, then, is to follow the example of the Savior. He is to become an agent of sanctification, working with the Holy Spirit to encourage her to grow toward maturity in Christ. He will need to be a model of righteousness. He will need to lead her not into temptation but to point her away from sin. He will provide her with opportunities to individually and together learn God's Word.

Nourish and Cherish

I was talking one evening to Charlie, a dentist friend of mine, who told me about a quest he was on. "I have decided," he announced, "to reclaim Sunday morning."

He continued. "Here's what I do. I get up at 7:00 A.M. I try to allow my hardworking and devoted wife one morning of extra sleep. She needs it. While everyone else sleeps, I dress and shave and have a good quiet time. I read a chapter from Proverbs and a few psalms. Sometimes I whisper a psalm back to the Lord.

"I resist the temptation to get the newspaper out of the driveway or to turn on the TV. The next thing I do is to wake up the children. I go sit on the side of their beds, and I rub their backs and cuddle with them and tell them I love them. I remind them that breakfast will be on the table at 9:00 A.M. sharp, and they need to be dressed and have their beds made if they want anything to eat.

"While they are busy, I go to work on breakfast—scrambled eggs and toast, or pancakes, or whatever. Usually, the activity around the house wakes my sleeping wife, who begins to get herself ready for church. Along with the kids, she arrives at the table for breakfast. But I don't stop there. While everyone eats, I will find something to read—a passage from the Bible, and maybe a story from the *Book of Virtues*. After breakfast, we all pitch in to clean the kitchen, and by quarter to ten, we're ready for church.

"This has beaten the socks off our former pattern of running around scolding each other, saying 'We're going to be late if you don't hurry,' and 'You are always late. You need to think of others. Someday, I may just go off and leave you.' We used to fuss at each other until we were at the point of tears. No more.

"You know what?" my friend asked. "This one simple act has had a big impact on our family. While I'm getting breakfast, my wife gets a little extra sleep and some time alone in the bathroom to do whatever magic she has to do on Sunday morning. She has not had to get a house full of kids dressed and fed while her husband reads the sports. She has been made to feel special. The very first act of the week, every week, honors her and sets her on the high place that she deserves."

Charlie's quest to reclaim Sunday morning for his family is just one way in which he nourishes and cherishes his wife.

When Paul challenges men to "nourish" their wives, he uses a unique word. In fact, the word for "nourish," *ektrepho*, is only found one other place in the Bible. A few verses later, Paul tells men not to exasperate their children but to "bring them up [*ektrepho*] in the discipline and instruction of the Lord" (Eph. 6:4).

Is a husband to "bring up" his wife? Does that mean he should treat her as one of the children? The answer, in a special sense, is yes. But he is not to think of his wife as a child. Nor is he to relate to her as a child. She is his partner. She does not need to be brought to maturity the way a child does. The Bible teaches here that a husband is responsible for his wife's ongoing spiritual, mental and emotional growth. She is in his care, and he is to shepherd her.

Now, we think of nourishment in physical terms. We provide nourishment for someone when we give him or her healthy food to eat. The word *ektrepho* carries that same meaning. But Paul expands on the idea. A man should not only nourish his wife by being a provider who makes sure there is healthy food for her to eat, but he also should nourish her soul. For his children, he nourishes them in the discipline and admonition of the Lord. He knows that man does not live by bread alone.

The old Puritan preachers knew this well. They would remind men that failure to provide for the physical needs of their families made them worse than the pagans (see 1 Tim. 5:8). But what good does it do, they would ask, if we care for their bodies but neglect their souls? Should we work diligently to satisfy their material and physical needs in this life, and to take no regard for their souls, which will live forever?

Paul reminds husbands that we are quick to satisfy our own need for nourishment. We rarely neglect our own bodies. Our care for our wife's needs should be just as acute. We are to labor to provide nourishment for her body, and we are to strive to provide nourishment for her soul.

Charlie's Sunday morning breakfast quite literally provides his family with nourishment, while it sets the tone for their corporate worship of God later that same morning. While he is meeting his wife's physical need for nourishment, he is also nourishing her emotionally and spiritually by sacrificing for her. Each week, as he takes one day and frees her from her normal routine, he is honoring her.

A wife is not only to be nourished; she is also to be cherished. Once again, Paul uses a unique word, *thalpo*. It shows up only one other time in the New Testament. There, he reminds his readers that he and his fellow missionaries had "proved to be gentle among you, as a nursing mother *tenderly cares* [*thalpo*] for her own children" (1 Thess. 2:7, emphasis added).

A husband, then, is to tenderly care for his wife in the same way that a mother gently and tenderly cares for a new baby. As a father of five, I've had a lot of opportunity to observe the special bond that grows between a mother and her child. After each child was born, I would watch as Mary Ann spent hours caring for our new son or daughter. She could sit for what seemed like forever to me, stroking his hair with her hand, talking to him, reacting to every coo or every facial gesture the baby would make. Even in the middle of the night, when the child had awakened her from a few precious hours of rest, she would gently care for, nurse and talk to her baby. Her regular routines were interrupted, but it didn't matter. Nothing would get in the way of caring for the new little life in our home.

That's what it looks like to cherish someone. The word "cherish" literally means, "to soften or warm with body heat." It means we make another person our priority relationship. We cherish our wives by providing them with a warm, safe, secure environment, where they will never doubt our love, our care and our commitment.

Think of it this way. If I were to ask you to name your most cherished possession—the one you'd run into the house to save in a fire—you would begin to mentally sort through the things you own. You would quickly eliminate the things that are easily replaceable. If you can buy the same item at Wal-Mart for under 10 dollars, it's not likely to appear on your cherished possession list.

You would slowly begin to narrow the list down to a few items. All of them would either be very expensive or perhaps irreplaceable. There would also very likely be some kind of emotional attachment to the items on your list—something that tied them to a special time or a special person in your life. If you were finally able to narrow the list down to a single item, it would very likely be something you alone would find valuable. Your cherished possessions are a unique part of your life.

That list of valued possessions gives us a taste of what it means to cherish our wife. She is highly valued. She is our priority. She is cared for. We ought to regularly reflect back to her how cherished she is.

Many husbands express their love for their wives with a big event or lavish gifts: a cruise, a trip to Europe, expensive jewelry and so on. Husbands know how to go all out with the spectacular displays of love. Yet can they sacrifice to do the little things that show their wives that they cherish them day after day?

The big events all play a part in expressing our affection for our wives. However, unless we are doing the little things that say, "I cherish you," every day, the big events ring hollow. Our wives will come to resent the diamond bracelets or the dresses, if that's all there is. They will see them as an attempt to buy their affection. Cherishing our wives, and letting them know they are cherished, requires constant expressions of love and devotion.

Recently, we interviewed Pastor Tommy Nelson from Denton Bible Church in Denton, Texas, for our radio program *FamilyLife Today*. Tommy has gained notoriety in the Dallas area for a series of messages he gave to a singles Bible study, taken from the Song of Solomon. During the interview, Tommy described romance as a "marriage discipline." A husband may have some natural abilities or instincts in that direction, he said. During courtship, these natural instincts flow freely. But in marriage we have to refine our instincts and abilities through regular romance workouts. We can't rely on our spontaneous romantic urges to communicate our devotion for our wives.

He's right. I need to let my wife know that I cherish her, and I need to find ways to do it regularly and creatively. They don't need to be expensive or extravagant; they simply need to be genuine and regular.

One night several years ago, after Mary Ann had gone to bed, I took a notepad and a pen and sat down at the kitchen table to write her a series of short, one-line love notes. Each one said something very simple: "I'm glad you're my wife"; "I love you very much"; "I still find you wildly attractive." Once the notes were written, I went to work. I placed them strategically all over the house. One was in a spot where she would see it the next day. Another was tucked away in her Bible. A third was put in a recipe file in the kitchen. And so on.

For the next few weeks and months, the notes continued to pop up in unexpected places—glove compartment, mailbox, fine china cabinet. That one night of note writing sent its message for weeks to come. In fact, the one in the recipe file is still where I put it, more than a decade ago—not because Mary Ann hasn't found it, but because she has left it right where I put it!

A husband nourishes his wife by caring for her physical, spiritual and emotional needs. He shows her that he cherishes her when he makes her a priority and regularly expresses his affection, his devotion and his commitment to her.

The Bible reminds us as husbands that we ought to care for our wives as we care for our own flesh. The reason? She is! We have entered into a "one-flesh" relationship with her. Charles Hodge put it this way:

> It is just as unnatural for a man to hate his wife, as it would be for him to hate himself or his own body. A man may have a body that does not altogether suit him. He may wish it were hand-somer, healthier, stronger, or more active. Still it is his body, it is himself; and he nourisheth it and cherisheth it as tenderly as though it were the best and loveliest man ever had. So a man may have a wife whom he could wish to be better, or more beau-tiful, or more agreeable; still she is his wife, and by the constitu-tion of nature and ordinance of God, a part of himself. In neglecting or ill-using her he violates the laws of nature as well as the law of God. . . . If a husband and wife are one flesh, the husband must love his wife, "for no man ever yet hated his own flesh, but nourisheth and cherisheth it."[4]

In Closing

A commitment to love our wives involves not only proactive, self-sacrificing love, but also the responsibility of being an agent of sanctification in our wives' lives. The goal of our love is to see our wives become more like Christ. We must be ready to die to self as we cleanse her, nourish her and cherish her. This is no job for some mushy, romantic, hormone-crazed, self-absorbed man. Only real men need apply. Are you up to the challenge?

PointstoConsider

1. Read Ephesians 5:25-30 and write down the different ways a husband is to show his love for his wife.

   - What do you think it means to "sanctify" your wife?
   - What do you think it means to "nourish" her?
   - What do you think it means to "cherish" her?

2. What is the difference between *pleasing* your wife and *loving* your wife?

3. Read Hebrews 10:24. What are some ways you can encourage your wife "to love and good deeds"?

4. One way to encourage your wife in godly behavior is through your model and example of the spiritual life. As you look back over your years together, what are some examples of times when you provided a good model for your wife?

5. What were some times when you provided a bad model? How did that influence your wife?

6. Why do men often stop nourishing and cherishing their wives as years pass by?

7. What are some ways you can nourish your wife—physically and spiritually—over the next two weeks?

8. What are some ways you can let your wife know that you cherish her over the next two weeks?

EPILOGUE

"Mr. Lepine?"

"Yes?"

"I have the results back from our Human Relations Department
. . . are you still interested in the position, even after all I've
explained to you?"

"I think so. I mean, yes. Yes, I am. I know it's a big job, and I also
know I've got a lot to learn, but I want this job like no job I've
ever wanted in my life."

"Mr. Lepine, I am pleased to offer you a position as a husband."

"Really? Are you kidding?"

"No, I'm not kidding."

"I can't believe it! Really? This is great!"

"Congratulations."

"Thanks! I really thought I was out of the running after that last
part about loving your wife. I still can't believe I got the job!"

"You know, Mr. Lepine, we're not offering you this position
because you're qualified for it."

"I know, I know. I thought I was qualified before I got here, but it didn't take long for me to realize how mistaken I was. I mean, I may be slow, but I'm not stupid. Man!"

"Now, Mr. Lepine, this is a lifetime position. You understand that, right? I mean, if you get bored or restless a few years from now, that's tough. You're committed to this job for the rest of your life."

"I understand."

"We haven't talked about benefits, have we?"

"No, I guess we haven't . . ."

"As you know, there is no salary. There are other benefits, however. Sit down, and I'll go over a few of them with you . . ."

ENDNOTES

Chapter One

1. Robert Lewis, *Raising a Modern Day Knight* (Colorado Springs, CO: Focus on the Family, 1997).
2. George Gilder, *Men and Marriage* (Gretna, LA: Pelican Publishing Company, 1986). Although Gilder's book is not centered in Scripture, his insights into the nature of men rings true.
3. Only recently have ardent feminists been forced to admit that some sexual stereotypes are hard to train out of men and women. Note the *Newsweek* article "My Turn" from the week of October 29, 1996. Also, Ellen Fein and Sherrie Schneider, authors of the best-selling book *The Rules: Time-Tested Secrets for Capturing the Heart of Mr. Right* (Warner Books, 1996), have had to concede that although their advice for women goes against feminist dogma (i.e., "Never call a man" and "Smile, but wait for him to say hello first"), the rules seem to work for some reason that transcends the feminist agenda.

Chapter Two

1. Mike Mason, *The Mystery of Marriage* (Portland, OR: Multnomah Publishers, 1985), p. 26.
2. J. Madeleine Nash, "Is Sex Really Necessary?" *Time* (January 20, 1992), p. 47.
3. I can't resist pointing out here that God did not curse Adam and Eve, although we commonly hear people talk about "the curse" as men and women continue to struggle in life. The increase of pain in childbirth and the desire of a wife to rule over her

husband (which will be discussed later in the book) are *consequences of the Fall but are not a curse* from God. Similarly, the fact that the ground would be harder to manage and cultivate was a consequence of the Fall for Adam but was not a curse from God. The man and the woman were chastened by God but were not cursed.

4. Additionally, I believe the increased pain in childbirth is not only a reference to the physical pain of bearing children, but the emotional pain experienced by a mother (more than by a father) as she raises that child to maturity. This is part of the pain Eve experienced when Cain slew Abel.

5. George Gilder, *Men and Marriage* (Gretna, LA: Pelican Publishing Company, 1986), p. 26.

6. Unless otherwise noted, the biological information that follows is taken from Gregg Johnson, "The Biological Basis for Gender-Specific Behavior," quoted in John Piper and Wayne Grudem, eds., *Recovering Biblical Manhood and Womanhood: A Response to Evangelical Feminism* (Westchester, IL: Crossway Books, 1991), chapter 16.

7. Gregory L. Vistica and Stacy Sullivan, "At War Over Women," *Newsweek* (May 12, 1997), p. 49.

8. Gilder, *Men and Marriage*, p. 31.

9. Ibid., pp. 20–21.

Chapter Three

1. Larry Crabb, Don Hudson and Al Andrews, *The Silence of Adam* (Grand Rapids, MI: Zondervan Publishing Company, 1995), p. 32.

2. John Piper, *Future Grace* (Portland, OR: Multnomah Publishers, 1995), n.p.

3. Dennis Rainey, *One Home at a Time* (Colorado Springs, CO: Focus on the Family, 1997), n.p.

4. Don McCullough, *The Trivialization of God* (Colorado Springs, CO: NavPress, 1995), p. 93.

5. Frederica Matthewes-Green, "All Things Considered: Men Protecting Women," *National Public Radio* (October 9, 1996).

6. Douglas Phillips, "Titanic Chivalry," *World Magazine* (March 28, 1998), pp. 28–29.

7. Ibid.

Chapter Four

1. I'd suggest to those who want to begin a discipline of Bible reading that you select a translation of the Bible like the *New International Readers Version*, the *New Century Version* or the *New Living Bible*. Look for special editions of these Bibles that are designed for those who want to read the Bible through in one year.

2. Be careful to note that most study Bibles will reflect certain theological biases about the Scriptures. The *Scofield Study Bible*, for example, will interpret some passages very differently from the *New Geneva Study Bible*. Ask your pastor for a recommendation before you purchase a study Bible.

3. Again, a caution. Some Bible commentaries may take a liberal view of Scripture, suggesting miracles didn't really happen or other ideas that undermine our trust in God's unfailing Word. Before making a purchase, ask your pastor for a suggestion on commentaries and dictionaries.

4. Paul and Susie Luchsinger's story is found in their book *A Tender Road Home: The Story of How God Healed a Marriage Crippled by Anger and Abuse* (Nashville, TN: Broadman and Holman Publishers, 1999), n.p.

Chapter Five

1. Don Whitney, *Spiritual Disciplines for the Christian Life* (Colorado Springs, CO: NavPress, 1991), n.p. I also encourage readers to read Ken Hughes's book *Disciplines of a Godly Man* (Westchester, IL: Crossway Books, 1995).
2. Saint Augustine, *Confessions*, vol. VIII, p. 29.
3. C. S. Lewis, "Work or Prayer," *God in the Dock* (Grand Rapids, MI: Eerdmans Publishing Company, 1970), p. 105.
4. Robert Robinson; adapted by Margaret Clarkson from the hymn "Come, Thou Fount of Every Blessing."
5. Chuck Colson with Ellen Santilli Vaughn, *The Body* (Dallas, TX: Word, 1992), p. 32.
6. Ibid., p. 70.
7. Ibid.

Part Two: The Model for Husbands: Jesus Christ

1. Wayne Grudem offers a detailed theological examination of the debate over the meaning of the Greek word *Kephale* in an appendix to the book *Recovering Biblical Manhood and Womanhood: A Response to Evangelical Feminism* (Westchester, IL: Crossway Books, 1991), n.p.
2. John Calvin, *The Institutes of the Christian Religion*, trans. Henry Beveridge (Grand Rapids, MI: Eerdmans Publishing Company, 1993), pp. 425–426.

Chapter Six

1. Richard Owen Roberts, ed., *Sanctify the Congregation* (Wheaton, IL: International Awakening Press, 1994), p. 24.
2. Jerry Marcellino, *Rediscovering the Lost Treasure of Family Worship* (Laurel, MS: Audubon Press, 1996), n.p.
3. Samuel Davies, *The Godly Family: A Series of Essays on the Duties of Parents and Children* (Pittsburgh, PA: Soli Deo Gloria Publications, 1993), p. 18.
4. J. I. Packer, *Knowing God* (Downers Grove, IL: InterVarsity Press, 1973), p. 22.
5. John Yates, *How a Man Prays for His Family* (Minneapolis, MN: Bethany House Publishers, 1996), p. 92.
6. Edythe Draper, *Draper's Book of Quotations for the Christian World* (Wheaton, IL: Tyndale House Publishers, 1992), entry 7196.

Chapter Seven

1. Dan Allender, "Mimicking Our Disruptive Father and Our Diverse Older Brother," *Mars Hill Review* 5 (Summer 1996), p. 41.
2. Douglas Wilson, *Reforming Marriage* (Moscow, IN: Canon Press, 1995), pp. 33–34.
3. Ibid., p. 32.

Chapter Eight

1. Dan Allender, "Mimicking Our Disruptive Father and Our Diverse Older Brother," *Mars Hill Review* 5 (Summer 1996), p. 44.

2. I might even suggest here that we would be better off referring to husbands as "loving leaders" rather than servant leaders. Our role as husbands is ultimately to serve God. In saying that, I am not trying to free us as husbands from any of our biblical responsibilities but to steer us away from potential compromise to God done in the name of "serving" our mate. Remember, the person to whom we are married is as tainted by sin as we are. "Serving" her should never be an excuse for allowing her to indulge her own selfishness.

3. The same phrase is found in the next chapter, when God is speaking to Cain following the murder of Abel. "Sin is crouching at the door; and *its desire is for you*, but you must master it (Gen. 4:7, emphasis added). In that context, the meaning is perfectly clear.

4. C. F. Keil and F. Delitzsch, *Commentary on the Old Testament*, vol. 1 (Grand Rapids, MI: Eerdmans Publishing Company, 1983), n.p.

5. *The Quest for Authentic Manhood* is an excellent film series on manhood produced by Robert Lewis. For more information on the series, call Fellowship Bible Church of Little Rock, Arkansas, at (501) 224-7171.

6. Dan Allender and Tremper Longman III, *Intimate Allies* (Wheaton, IL: Tyndale House Publishers, 1995), p. 89.

7. Allender, "Mimicking Our Disruptive Father and Our Diverse Older Brother," *Mars Hill Review*, p. 44.

Chapter Nine

1. Richard Selzer, *Mortal Lessons: Notes on the Art of Surgery* (New York: A Harvest Bode, Harcourt, Inc., 1996), n.p.

2. Editorial, "Couples Without Vows, 1978-1998," *Indianapolis News,* July 30, 1998, sec. A.

3. Robertson McQuilkin, "Living by Vows," *Christianity Today* (October 8, 1990), quoted in Stuart and Jill Briscoe, eds., *The Family Book of Christian Values* (Colorado Springs, CO: Chariot Victor, 1995), p. 43.

Chapter Ten

1. Charles Hodge, *Commentary of the First Epistle to the Corinthians* (Grand Rapids, MI: Eerdmans Publishing Company, 1976), p. 269.

2. R. C. H. Lenski quoted in John MacArthur, *First Corinthians: The MacArthur New Testament Commentary* (Chicago: Moody Press, 1984), p. 345.

3. H. A. Ironside, *The First Epistle to the Corinthians* (Neptune, NJ: Loizeaux Brothers, 1938), pp. 428-429.

4. John MacArthur, *First Corinthians: The MacArthur New Testament Commentary*, pp. 353–354.

5. Roy Laurin, *First Corinthians: Where Life Matures* (Grand Rapids, MI: Kregel Publications, 1987), p. 237.

Chapter Eleven

1. John MacArthur, *Ephesians: The MacArthur New Testament Commentary* (Chicago: Moody Press, 1986), p. 300.

2. James M. Boice, *Ephesians: An Expositional Commentary* (Grand Rapids, MI: Zondervan Publishing Company, 1996), p. 176.

3. John MacArthur, *Family Feuding: How to End It* study notes (Panorama City, CA: Word of Grace Communications, 1981), p. 55.

4. Charles Hodge, *Commentary on the Epistle to the Ephesians* (Grand Rapids, MI: Eerdmans Publishing Company, 1966), p. 33.

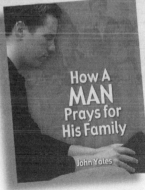
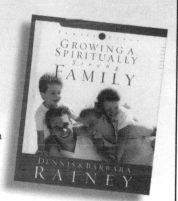